101
ANGLES for FRESH-WATER and DOCK
FISHING

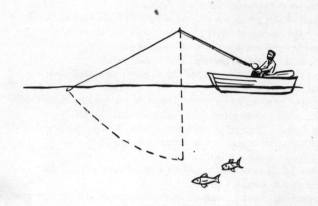

By GIL PAUST
ILLUSTRATIONS BY DWIGHT DOBBINS

501

STERLING PUBLISHING CO., Inc.   New York

Glossary

Anadromous: Pertaining to fish that are born in fresh water, live in salt water, then return to fresh water to spawn.

Backlash: A tangle of line on a bait-casting reel caused when the spool is allowed to overrun because it is not thumbed.

Bait-Casting: A fishing method which uses a short, stiff rod and a multiplying reel with revolving spool and handle.

Barbel: A whisker or feeler growing from the corner of the mouth of certain fish species, such as Catfish and Carp.

Bobber: A small float used to hold a baited hook off the bottom and to indicate to the angler when a fish bites.

Brackish: Water which is a mixture of salt and fresh, such as that found near the mouths of rivers emptying into a bay or ocean.

Chum: Bait thrown into the water to attract fish.

Chum Slick: A trail of chum in a current of water.

Dipsey: A type of sinker shaped like a drop, heavy at the base.

Dorsal: Top fin of a fish.

Drag: Device to hold firm the line spool on a spinning or spin-casting reel; adjustable to protect the line against a fish's pull.

Drop Line: A hand line, consisting of line, bobber, sinker and hook without a rod or reel; fish is pulled in by hand.

Dry Fly: An imitation fly that floats.

Feather Jig: A salt-water lure with a metal head and a feather body intended to imitate a minnow.

Ferrule: The joint by means of which two sections of a fishing rod are joined.

Fly-Casting: A fishing method designed to cast an almost weightless artificial fly and leader.

Gaff: A long-handled, large barbless hook used to spear and land large fish when a regular landing net would be too small.

Guides: Rings on a rod through which the line passes.

Gunwale: The inside strip around the top of a boat.

Copyright © 1961 by
Sterling Publishing Co., Inc.
419 Fourth Avenue, New York 16, N.Y.
Manufactured in the United States of America
Library of Congress Catalog Card No.: 61-10407

Hellgrammite: Large black insect with nippers, larva of the Dobson fly; good bait for fresh-water panfish, Black Bass, etc.

Jig: When still-fishing, to work a bait up and down a short distance continually to attract fish.

Larva: Beetle-like form of an insect before it turns into a flying form.

Leader: A strand of thin nylon used as an invisible connection between a line and its lure; also, a short wire connection between line and lure to resist a fish's teeth.

Lunker: Any especially large fish that might be considered a trophy.

Lure: A bait or decoy to fool fish.

Monofilament: Single-strand nylon line.

Nymphs: Underwater larva forms of insects.

Panfish: A small fish of frying-pan size.

Plugs: Wooden or plastic lures which imitate (at least vaguely) some minnow on which the fish feeds.

Rig: Equipment.

School: A crowd of fish of the same species.

Shiners: Live bait; minnows; small bait-fish.

Shoal: Shallow area in a body of water.

Silt: Fine earth or sand carried and deposited by a current of water.

Sinker: A lead weight which can be added to line for casting, carrying a lure deeper, and anchoring a baited hook for still-fishing.

Snell: A short leader (10 to 12 inches) tied to a hook with a loop on its other end.

Snelled Fly: A fly with a snell attached.

Spin-Casting: A casting method that uses a special spin-cast reel; not spinning.

Spinning: A method of casting light lures using a fixed-spool reel and a light nylon line (thread-line).

Split-Shot: A type of sinker which is a lead BB or buckshot split almost in half; it is squeezed together to hold line.

Stink Bait: A smelly bait of various materials (old cheese, insides of animals and chickens, animal blood, etc.) used as bait for Catfishing.

Stone Fly: A type of nymph, or insect larva.

Tippet: The end, and finest, section of a tapered leader, the weakest and most invisible part which is tied to the fly.

Torpedo Taper: A line which consists of three widths: narrowest at the end that is tied to the fly, followed by the thickest section which provides weight for the cast, then by the rest of the line which is slightly heavier than the light section.

Trolling: A fishing method in which a lure or bait is towed behind a boat.

Wet Fly: An artificial fly designed to resemble a drowned insect.

Wobbler: A lure that wobbles, or zig-zags, through the water.

Contents

Foreword

Whether you're a beginner or an old-timer—a worm-dunker, plug-tosser or a dry-fly puritan—this book will tell you many things you'll want to know to get the most out of your fishing. And it will do it in plain fish-talk so you can't miss.

For example, it will tell you about the most popular kinds of fresh-water and dock-side game fish, where to find them and how to catch them. I don't mean how to catch them *only* when they're biting. You'll see that this is no trick once you know their favorite chow and how to offer it to them on the right hook or lure without making them suspicious. You will learn how to catch these fish when they *aren't* biting (which will probably seem to be most of the time). Much of this is angling savvy that seldom gets into print because the old backwoodsmen and guides and salt-water professionals prefer to keep it to themselves.

Here you will also learn about the different ways you can go fishin', the various methods and tackle, so you won't have to confine your fun to just one kind. You'll be able to try them all.

The first two sections of the book tell you about the most popular fresh- and salt-water fish and how to fool them. Then you will learn about the various fishing methods—fly-casting, bait-casting, spinning and so forth. You can use more than one method for the kind of fish you are going after, of course. The choice is up to you, but you will find that varying your methods provides the most fun—and the most fish. The last section covers the different kinds of bait. If you come across a word or term that is unfamiliar, check the glossary.

But even when you don't catch fish, goin' fishin' is fun. Being out on a stream or pond or bay with a rod and reel, knowing that somewhere under the surface a big "lunker" may be lurking, waiting just for you, makes your pulse pound and gives you a thrill nothing else can. If you don't catch him, so what? You might the next time.

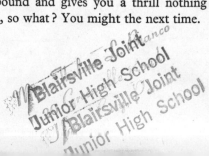

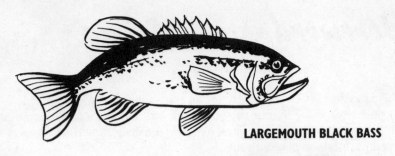

LARGEMOUTH BLACK BASS

SMALLMOUTH BLACK BASS

ROCK BASS

CRAPPIE

6

Part 1—

Fresh-Water Game Fish and How to Fool Them

LARGEMOUTH BLACK BASS

This big fresh-water tacklebuster is a favorite of anglers because of his savagery when he attacks a lure, and because of his head-shaking, leaping battle when hooked. Due to transplanting, he now can be found in ponds, lakes and rivers throughout the United States, and even in Canada, Mexico, Germany, Spain, France and Africa. His general color is greenish-bronze on the back, a lighter green on the sides, and yellow-white on the belly. A line of black marks extends along each of his sides from jaw to tail, giving him the name "Linesides." An easy way to distinguish him from his close relative, the Smallmouth Black Bass, is by the joint of his closed jaw which lies to the rear of his eye, while in the Smallmouth it is directly below the eye. The Largemouth averages 2 pounds in Northern waters, 8 pounds down South. The world record is 22 pounds, 4 ounces.

The easiest time to catch him is at daybreak and dusk; the best place is close to shore, especially near lily pads, underwater rocky lairs and large surface snags such as fallen trees. He enters this shallow water during the night to hunt for minnows and fry (young fish), night-crawlers that may have slipped off the bank, frogs, lizards, field mice and, in fact, any living thing that can fit into his cavernous mouth, which is large enough to hold another fish two-thirds his own size. Bass have been known to gobble baby ducks, and even to try to swallow one of the parents!

Under these conditions, any of the above natural foods can be used to catch him. But none of them is necessary. When Bass are feeding at sunup and sundown, they'll grab almost anything. So, use artificial lures. The lures that "swim" on the surface or just below it are the best since they aren't likely to get "hung up," or snagged, on bottom grass or rocks. Besides, the strike of a Bass at a surface lure is spectacular, a thrill you'll long remember. You don't need a leader to connect your line to the lure. Tie the line to it directly or attach it with a small snap-swivel. Use bait-casting or medium-weight spinning tackle and nylon line of at least 8-pound-test (breaking strength).

Shortly after daybreak, as the sun begins to warm the shallows, the Largemouth Bass stops feeding and moves to deeper water, not returning until late evening when he works his way shoreward again for his nightly hunt for food. Bass fishing during the day, when the sun is high and the Bass are deep, usually mystifies anglers. They don't know how to find Bass in deep water! And even when they find them, they can't get them to strike! "The Bass aren't feeding," is the old excuse. Maybe so, but if the only Bass caught were those that were feeding, there would be many more empty stringers. Catching a feeding Bass at dawn or dusk is comparatively easy; catching a non-feeding Bass at midday can be almost as easy—if you remember (1) he's the biggest bully in the lake, and (2) it's easy to get him to prove it!

To find Bass in deep water, first find a submerged weed bed. The Bass will be hiding in it. To find the weed bed, drag a treble-hook on a line-and-sinker from the rear of your boat until it snags fresh weeds. Then back off to within casting distance, anchor your boat, and cast to the weed bed with a deep-swimming lure.

The Bass's bully instinct is his downfall. For a century the most successful Bass lure has been a plug with a red head and white body. Can you guess why? Fish, unlike many animals, aren't color blind. When the flash of a plug's white body attracts a dozing Bass, it draws

his attention to the red head. And in his world, red signifies only one thing—blood. The red on the white minnow means it has been injured, and an injured minnow can't swim fast enough to escape even a lazy Bass; it's an easy prey. Should he snap it up? The bully in him begins to stir.

Maybe the first few times he'll let the "cripple" swim by. Keep casting to the same spot, retrieving the plug in sharp jerks to simulate injury even more authentically. Every time he sees this teaser stagger past his nose, he'll fin a little faster. Eventually, the bully in him takes over. He comes in a rush—and you've a fight on your hands.

Remember, when there doesn't seem to be a sign of a Bass anywhere, go to deep water over a weed bed with a red-and-white plug or a red-and-silver spoon. Add a sinker to the line ahead of it to sink it deeper, if necessary. Give it lots of "wounded" action, and cast at least a dozen times to the same spot before shifting to a new one a few yards to the right or left. If you don't get a Largemouth then, it will be because there aren't any left in the lake!

SMALLMOUTH BLACK BASS

The Smallmouth Black Bass (average weight: 1½ pounds; world record: 11 pounds, 15 ounces) may not be as large as his Largemouth cousin, in over-all size as well as jaw-spread, but he makes up for it in scrappiness. When a Smallmouth feels your hook he will treat you to a dazzling display of acrobatics and headshaking that usually unhooks your lure and tosses it back at you. Fishermen for Smallmouth will tell you that you have to know more than just fishing; you have to be able to duck fast, too.

The Smallmouth, like the Largemouth, can be found almost everywhere in the United States, due to transplanting, but he's at his fightin' best in the cold, invigorating waters of the Northeastern states and Southern Canada. In appearance he resembles the Largemouth also, although his green back and sides may have an even richer bronze sheen, giving him the nickname "Bronzeback." The distinguishing difference, of course, is his mouth. The joint of his closed jaw lies directly below his eye, not behind it as in the Largemouth. And sometimes each of his eyes will contain a red spot, which is a clue to his fiery disposition.

The Smallmouth likes clear, cold water and he prefers it to be moving. In a lake you'll find him over sand bars and rocky bottoms, not over mud bottoms and only occasionally in weed beds. He migrates into shallow water during the night to dine, but the shallows he chooses are those fed by springs or nearby streams. Look for him at dawn and dusk along rocky shores, and especially in the deep mouths of feeder streams. If the stream is large and deep enough, you'll usually find him there rather than in the lake itself. As a general rule, you'll find Largemouth Bass in the lake, and Trout and Smallmouth Bass in the river that feeds it, the Trout occupying the fast, tumbling waters of the rapids and the Smallmouth Bass the slower, deep water of the "runs" between the rapids.

The Smallmouth's menu is more limited than that of the Largemouth. He likes minnows, frogs and the occasional worms, insects, crawfish and hellgrammites (the larvae of large insects) the stream washes down to his waiting mouth, which isn't quite as small as his name implies. At dawn and dusk when he's hungry, he's just as hungry as his Largemouth cousin. But he's more discriminating. He prefers to look your lure over once or twice before taking it instead of gobbling it blindly. And a live minnow or frog or worm, with a big hook on it and dangled on a heavy line, or a big lure bristling with hooks, won't fool him very often in spite of any red color you might add to it. Use small, noisy surface lures with your bait-casting or spinning outfits, and with the former use a yard-long 10-pound-test nylon leader between line and lure so he won't see that they're connected. For the most thrills, try catching him on a heavy fly rod (about 5 ounces), with an 8-pound-test leader on your line, and floating lures that resemble night-flying moths—the kind of lures called "popping bugs" that have concave heads and "pop" along the surface when you retrieve them in jerks. Red-and-white are the best colors, with deer-hair "wings." And how the Bass love to smash them!

Since the Smallmouth is discriminating when he's feeding, as you might guess he's quite difficult to fool when he isn't feeding! First find him! Since he prefers cool water, during the heat of the day he'll be deep, haunting the dark sand bars and rock-strewn bottoms at 20- to 100-foot depths. "Feel" the bottom with a sinker (about 2 ounces) on your line, trailed behind your boat. If weeds tug at your sinker, move on! When your sinker hits a rocky bar, you'll feel it bounce from one rock to the next. Try there! Sand bars in a lake are more difficult to spot. Many of them, like rocky bars, extend far out into deep water from a projecting point of land. Best solution here is to inquire; learn their location from the local fishermen or game warden.

Deep-swimming red-and-white lures, used as for Largemouth Bass— in injured minnow fashion, many times over the same spot—will coax a Smallmouth, too, because he's also a bully like his cousin. But frequently it's more effective to capitalize on this Smallmouth weakness in another way. Tie a small silver spinner-and-hook onto your line about 2 feet ahead of your deep-swimming lure, cast, and retrieve the combination in long, fast jerks. What does the Smallmouth see swimming by? A large minnow chasing a small silver one! Keep casting, and after he has been confronted with this tempting scene a few times, he soon becomes convinced that here's a bargain he shouldn't overlook. And no matter which he grabs—the minnow that's doing the chasing or the one that's being chased—you hook him either way.

To keep him from throwing the lure back at you when he jumps

after you've hooked him, keep a tight line on him! As he starts to break water, lean back on your rod tip to turn him over. This pressure will keep him on—most of the time.

ROCK BASS AND CRAPPIE

The Rock Bass and Crappie (pronounced "Croppie") are two of our most popular "panfish," so called because most of those we catch are just about the right size for our frying pans—about $\frac{1}{2}$ pound. But 2-pounders are common and the world record Crappie weighed in at 5 pounds, 3 ounces; the largest Rock Bass reported was almost 4 pounds.

It isn't their taste that makes these fish so popular, however. Even skinned and fried in butter, they can't match the mouth-watering flavor of fresh Trout, or even Pickerel. The reason for their popularity is mainly that there are so many of them! Once they start hitting your lure, the action is fast and furious. You can collect enough for a dozen frying pans as fast as you can pull them in. Which still isn't enough, according to conservationists. They complain that anglers don't catch enough of them, and that these species breed so fast that they eat up all the available food and starve out the larger species such as Trout and Black Bass. This is, of course, a happy situation for the angler who loves panfish. And for the non-hungry fisherman who just enjoys the excitement of the sport, both Rock Bass and Crappie, when hooked on a rod that's light enough and resilient enough to give them a fighting chance, put up a scrap with plenty of thrills.

The Rock Bass gets his name from his chunky shape, which is like that of the Black Bass, and from his color. He is a dark olive-green, and each of his scales carries a black mark, giving him a spattered appearance like that of an underwater rock lying among the weeds. Because of his red-rimmed eyes, he's sometimes called "Redeye." The Crappie is more tapered in shape and lighter in color, his green back and upper sides carrying a mottled black shading while his lower sides and belly are almost colorless with no markings. And he has a nickname, too: "Papermouth"—because his mouth is so tender your hook will pull out if you're not extra careful in playing him. Both species are found throughout the United States and Southern Canada, but you'll find the best Rock Bass waters in the Midwest. And in the South the Crappie is the "White Crappie"; in the North the "Black Crappie." The distinction is slight, however.

Both the Rock Bass and Crappie have similar habits although they're seldom found in the same body of water, mainly because one will soon eat the other to extinction. They thrive in mud-bottom lakes, slow streams and rivers, and even in your own back-yard pond if you give them enough feed and keep catching them so they won't die off from overcrowding. Because they're always hungry and feeding, they're always eager to take a bait or lure. Their menu includes all insects—flies, grasshoppers, crickets, worms, moths and hellgrammites—and fry and minnows one inch long or smaller. Any of these on a hook will be accepted. But artificials usually will do just as well. You can buy excellent imitation insects made of rubber, and small feathered floating bugs. For imitation flies use ordinary Trout flies—on dark days the brighter patterns such as Red Ibis and Royal Coachman, on bright days the dark flies such as the Black Gnat. For imitation minnows, there are a thousand small spinning lures to choose from. Almost all of them will fool panfish. But—for the most sport use the lightest tackle you can get! Try a fly rod or spinning rod that weighs less than 3 ounces, if you have one. Your fly-line leader should taper to 2X and your spinning line should be a 3-pound-test "thread-line" monofilament. Hooked on one of these combinations, a one-pound Redeye or Papermouth will make you think you've snagged a whale!

The secret of catching these fish is just to find them. They travel in schools, and the schools may be anywhere. Usually a bait-angler anchors his boat in a fishy spot, tosses his hook-and-line overboard and waits until the school works his way. Then he pulls in fish until the school leaves or is frightened away, after which he resumes his wait, hoping it will return. The fly-caster or spin-caster usually casts hit-or-miss, but when the fish are feeding on flies hatching on the water he has no trouble locating them. The surface around the hatch is covered with dimples, and each dimple is a Rock Bass or Crappie sucking in a fly.

But there's a simple method of locating a school, one you can use whether you bait-fish, fly-cast or spin-cast. You can attract the school to your boat or dock by using a trick of salt-water anglers. "Chum" them to you. For salt-water species, different substances are used but all you need for panfish is a loaf of white bread. Crumble a handful of bread into small pieces and toss it as far as possible into the water. The wind will help carry it out. As the bread sinks slowly in a white shower, the pieces will be visible for a long distance underwater and if the school

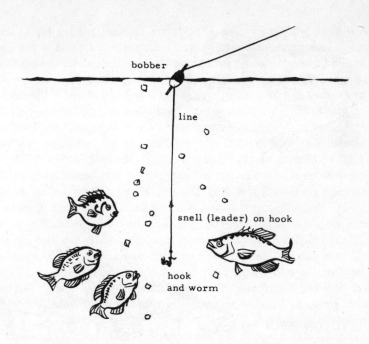

bobber

line

snell (leader) on hook

hook
and worm

is within sight, it will come to investigate. Throw out a few handfuls, wait a minute, then cast your bait, fly or spinning lure into the sinking "chum." If you don't get a strike in several casts, throw out more bread. When the school has moved in and has been striking, then starts to leave, stop casting and throw out more "chum" to bring them back. Keep your body low and play each fish carefully, quietly and slowly so you won't make a commotion to scare away the others.

BLUEGILL

YELLOW PERCH

WHITE PERCH

16

BLUEGILL AND SUNFISH

The Bluegill, also called Roach and Bream (pronounced "Brim"), and others of the Sunfish family are our most common panfish. These little battlers furnish many of us with our first fishing thrills, and even experienced anglers still find them fun to catch on the right tackle. They're not heavyweights—$\frac{1}{4}$-pounders are average and one-pounders rare—but experts agree that pound-for-pound they fight harder on a hook-and-line than any other fish in existence! The Pickerel with his long, torpedo-like body may be the underwater speed champ but the flat, disk-shaped Sunfish is built not only for speed but also for wheeling and darting. Moreover, a plump butter-fried Bluegill will make any angler's mouth water.

The Sunfish species are even more numerous than Rock Bass and Crappie. They can be found in almost all waters from coast to coast, the exceptions being the very fast and cold Trout streams of the Northern states, and those waters which contain other fish large enough to make a meal of the Sunfish, such as Black Bass and the Pickerel family. In recent years, Bluegill have become favorites of owners of small homemade ponds. If you stock a one-acre pond with Bluegill and feed it and fish it enough, perhaps adding a few Black Bass to help keep down the Bluegill population, it will produce over 200 pounds of fish per year for your dinner table! In addition to all the fun you'll have catching them!

The origin of the Sunfish's name is interesting. It was chosen because all of these species do their courting and breeding only when the sun is shining brightly. At that time their colors are most brilliant. But even when they're not breeding, Sunfish are the most colorful of all the fresh-water fishes. Major color variations, and slight physical differences, designate their various species. Popularity winner and second in beauty is the largest Sunfish—the Bluegill (world record: 4 pounds, 12 ounces). He is dark green with darker green vertical side bars, a brown-to-scarlet belly and an over-all purple iridescence. A jet-black tab projects from the end of each gill cover and his cheeks are an iridescent blue, which gives him his name. The top beauty is the Pumpkinseed, so called because the orange spots that dot his sides resemble in color and shape the seeds of a pumpkin. He is a deeper purple than the Bluegill, his belly is orange and his cheeks an even brighter orange with a brilliant red spot on each gill cover. In addition to the Bluegill and Pumpkinseed, there are: the Green Sunfish, which is colored like a Rock Bass; the Warmouth which looks like a Rock Bass but is slimmer and likes mud bottoms; the Shellcracker Sunfish with red-rimmed gill covers; the Yellowbelly Sunfish; the Long-eared Sunfish; and the brown Stumpknocker. And a few others. All of these species crossbreed, and the resulting young show quite confusing mixtures of colors which make their identity difficult. But Nature keeps the confusion from spreading further—the hybrids which result from these crossbreedings are incapable of producing young of their own.

Because Sunfish are so numerous, they must compete with each other for food and they're not choosey about their diet. They'll eat almost anything, although they have a special fondness for flies, grasshoppers and crickets. And, of course, worms when they can get them. Therefore you'll find that the shallows around the edge of a pond or lake are favorite haunts of Sunfish because there the insects fall into the water from the shore bushes and trees. But the exposed shallows during daylight can be dangerous, too, as when a hungry kingfisher or duck flies overhead. And so while he waits, watching for his dinner, the Sunny likes to remain hidden in the underwater weeds, or under a convenient lily pad. And there's another logical reason, besides food, for his preference for the sun and shore shallows—no Black Bass. During the day this archenemy of all panfish is content to remain in the deeper, cooler water and to let the Sunny have his way. Only the largest Bluegills retreat to deep weed beds during very hot weather.

Sunfish are easiest to catch in spring and fall when the males are guarding their spawning beds which they've scooped out of the sand in the quiet waters near shore. Then they attack anything to drive it away, even a big Black Bass lure that happens along. Catching them under these conditions might seem to be taking unfair advantage, but in most cases the spawning bed survives without the parent's protection—sometimes even better since he isn't around to gobble up the tiny fry as soon as they hatch.

Small spinning lures retrieved slowly, and both wet and dry Trout flies, will almost always catch Sunfish. And any good-sized insect baited on a hook will be sure to bring a Sunny on the run. But for the most sport, and also for an opportunity to test your casting skill, take

advantage of the Sunfish's lily-pad habit. Use a light fly rod (3 ounces or less), a leader that tapers to 2X, and a Trout fly or small imitation bug in fly-rod size. Cast the lure so that it lands directly on the lily pad. If you miss the pad and there's a Sunny hiding under it, he'll swim out and grab your offering. But it's more fun when you hit the pad. Then the Sunny will go crazy! You'll see him bump the pad with his nose, trying to shake off the fly or bug. And when this doesn't succeed, he'll jump right on top of the pad to sink it. Sometimes his splashing will bring some unexpected action—from a big, hungry Pickerel lurking in the nearby reeds. Then it's every man for himself!

YELLOW PERCH

It's fortunate for us that this little panfish isn't easily discouraged, and that he likes to raise large families, because he's pursued from all sides—by commercial fishermen as well as by sport-anglers. Look in the frozen food bin of any supermarket; you'll find "Yellow Perch Fillets" alongside the Lobster Tails and Shrimp. Over 6 million pounds of these fish are taken commercially every year from waters of the Great Lakes area. Add to this figure the unknown millions of pounds caught annually by sportsmen and you have a staggering total. But, miraculously, each year you'll find just as many Yellow Perch as previously. And they're always just as eager to snap up your lure and then try to snap your fishing rod.

If you're a resident of the Northeast, the Yellow Perch is your dish— to catch as well as to eat. He's found mainly from the Rockies east to the Atlantic and from the middle states north to Canada. Attempts to introduce him to the Pacific Coast failed. His favorite waters are large, deep lakes; most ponds are too small for him. When he's confined to a river with no lake on its course, he remains in the deep, quiet stretches. Once you've seen him you won't fail to recognize him the next time. He's a gaily colored fish—dark olive-green back, golden sides marked with 6 to 8 dark green vertical bars, and lower fins and tail tinted bright red. But he seems humpbacked due to a slight depression in the back of his head. In weight he averages one pound although in some waters he reaches 2 pounds. His unofficial world-record weight is 4 pounds, $3\frac{1}{2}$ ounces.

The Yellow Perch, like other panfish, eats anything that will fit in his mouth, and this includes insects of all kinds, worms, hellgrammites, crawfish and minnows. And artificial lures that look like them. He is a school fish like the Rock Bass and Crappie, but there are differences. In most instances Rock Bass and Crappie will wander all over a lake looking for food; a school of Yellow Perch will stay in deep water over a sandy or light-colored bottom, preferably near a thick weed bed that might shelter minnows and into which they can dart to hide if a marauding Black Bass should appear. And their food must come to them, either sinking down from the surface or crawling or swimming.

To catch any deep-water fish, even one as hungry as a Yellow

Perch, there are two requirements for success: (1) you must find the fish, and (2) you must get the bait or lure down to them so they can see it. Since the Yellow Perch lurks near deep weeds, find the school by first finding the deep weed bed. Do this by dragging a weighted treble hook behind your boat until it snags fresh weeds in 20 to 30 feet of water. Then anchor and cast your baited hook, spinning lure or fly *away* from the weed bed, not toward it as you would for Black Bass. Use a light fly rod of about 4 ounces—*glass*, not bamboo—and a fly line with a 3-foot leader of about 6-pound-test. Or try a 4-ounce spinning rod with 6-pound-test monofilament line. Realize that the lighter the rod, the more sport you'll have because the fish will be more difficult to tire and you'll have to play him more skillfully.

Your spinning lure is weighted and will sink down to the fish—if you give it a chance. After casting, count to 10 or more before starting to retrieve, then retrieve slowly. With each cast, vary the count to vary the depth to which the lure sinks, until you find the fish's level. Spinning lures that spin, not dart or wriggle, are best for Yellow Perch. When fly fishing for this fish you must weight the fly so it will sink quickly. Do this by twisting a short piece of "wrap-around" lead wire around the end of the fly line where it joins the leader, or by pinching a small lead split-shot on the leader just ahead of the fly. Cast, count and retrieve slowly, as recommended for spin-casting. Why a glass fly rod instead of one of split-bamboo? Because casting a weighted fly has strained and ruined many a fine, delicate—and expensive—bamboo fly rod. Only split-bamboo has the perfect action for precision casting of almost weightless Trout flies, but for general fly fishing, glass is tougher and cheaper.

Want to catch a "lunker" Yellow Perch? A big old "lunker" is smart and always suspicious of food that doesn't look just right. And while he's hesitating, one of his smaller brothers grabs it. He gets only what is too large for the others to swallow, which is plenty. So—go after him with a lure that's too large for the others—a spinner with a long, narrow, chromium-plated blade (about No. 5) that revolves close to the shaft. On the business end of the shaft put a large red-feathered treble hook, about No. 1. Once you've located a school of Yellow Perch in the deepest water by catching several, cast out this big spinner-and-feather, count so it can sink, then retrieve just fast enough to keep the blade turning. The "lunker" will think he sees a slow silver minnow his companions have injured and are chasing. Their excitement will bring him in a hurry. And to make sure he stays fooled even when he gets close to it, before casting place a piece of worm on each hook of the treble! Thread the worm on the hooks; if you drape it on, the smaller fish will pull it off. When the big Perch gets a snootful of this genuine appetizer, he'll be as good as hooked! A piece of worm on the tail of a fly or spinning lure, too, is always a good persuader when fish aren't biting with enthusiasm.

WHITE PERCH

Of the group of fish known as panfish, the White Perch has the distinction of being the most unusual. First, he's not really a Perch although in some ways he looks like one; biologists say he's really a Bass. Second, he sometimes grows so large he's a panfish only if you use a king-size frying pan. Third, he's "anadromous," which means he's equally at home in salt water or fresh water. He can live and breed contentedly in landlocked lakes which have no rivers connecting them with the ocean. And when you catch him there, he averages slightly over $\frac{1}{2}$ pound in weight. But when his home is a river emptying into the ocean, each year he migrates to the salt water to spend a vacation there, then swims back to his river to spawn. And the salt air seems to give him an appetite because after his trip he may weigh as much as 4 pounds. This gain in weight in salt water is true of all "anadromous" fish such as the Salmon and certain strains of Trout, notably the western Rainbow Trout which goes to sea and returns to his native river as a big "Steelhead."

The White Perch is slightly humpbacked like a Yellow Perch and his mouth is smaller than any Bass's. These features are partly responsible for the confusion over his name. But his body is deeper and much chunkier, similar to a Bass. In fresh water his color is silver with a greenish back but exposure to salt water bleaches the fish to an over-all brilliant silver. It also alters the flavor, due principally to the different diet. A lake or river White Perch has the sweet, delicate taste characteristic of the fresh-water panfish; fresh from the sea he is firm-fleshed and flavorful and claimed by many anglers to be the tastiest of bay fish.

The East Coast rivers and lakes are his home, from Newfoundland south to the Carolinas and west to the Allegheny Mountains. In lakes during summer and fall he haunts the deepest holes and the drop-offs near underwater ledges and rocky bars. If you know there are White Perch in a certain lake, you're sure to find them in these deep spots. To discover where these spots are, ask the local fishermen or game warden or sound for them yourself with a heavy sinker tied to a heavy fish line. In spring these landlocked White Perch usually spawn in the largest streams that feed the lake, and then you'll find them in the same fast water that Trout like, even at the foot of a rapids or waterfall if it is close to the lake itself. But seagoing White Perch aren't as easy to find. You won't find them at all while they're in the ocean. Where they go once they reach the Atlantic is a mystery no one has solved. They simply vanish! But they return during spring and summer, spawning in either the fresh water part of their river or in the "brackish" water where the salt water and fresh water mingle. They prefer this "brackish" water, and here the White Perch is not only large but a real tackle-buster, much stronger than his lake-reared relative. Look for him near the mouths of fresh-water streams that empty into the river, and in shallow bays which rise and fall with the tide. No matter where you catch him, however, either in fresh or salt water, the White Perch will give you lots of fishing fun because he has another happy characteristic of most panfish—he's a school fish, and when you catch one, you'll catch a dozen!

In fresh water, the White Perch feeds on conventional panfish fare: flies, insects, worms, small minnows and crawfish. In brackish water, he'll take small minnow-like baitfish, small crabs and shrimp, and earthworms, sandworms and bloodworms when you offer them. In a lake, he'll enthusiastically gobble artificial lures such as weighted flies, small spinners with feather-tail hooks, and spinning lures, all fished deep. If you use a fly rod, choose a glass one because this material isn't as likely to be damaged by the weighted flies as is split-bamboo. It should be light, about 4 ounces, with a 4-pound-test untapered fly-leader. For a spinning rod, a monofilament line of the same strength will be adequate.

Almost all brackish-water fishing for White Perch is done with bait, whether the angler fishes from a boat or dock. And the method is invariably the old hit-or-miss variety. He tosses out his baited hook and waits for a school to come, but frequently it never does. Here's how you can beat the bait-fisherman every time. Use a 5-ounce spinning rod, an 8-pound-test monofilament line and a small minnow-like silver spinning lure. By casting, you can cover more water area to find the fish. A school of White Perch 50 yards away from a stationary or drifting baited hook won't see it, but they can't miss the spinning lure you cast beyond them and retrieve in front of their noses. And seldom will they be so filled with food that they'll let it go by. Even when the school is beyond your casting range, the splash of the lure every time it hits the water will attract the fish, not scare them away. Once you've drawn in

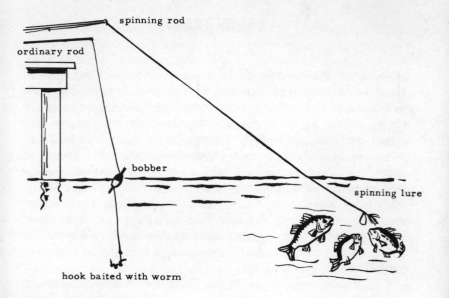

spinning rod

ordinary rod

bobber

spinning lure

hook baited with worm

the school, you won't have any trouble filling your bag. When they stop hitting, let the water rest for about a half-hour, then resume casting, this time with a different lure, one with red on it, and retrieve at a different speed. And if there are any bait-fishermen near you, make them thank you for helping them get their White Perch—it was your lure the fish were after!

BROOK TROUT

To biologists he's the Brook Trout, to Canadians he's the Speckled Trout, and to New Englanders he's the Squaretail, but no matter what he's called, to anglers everywhere he's the aristocrat of game fish. His haunts are the purest waters of picturesque mountain streams and crystal-clear lakes. He takes the angler's dry fly eagerly—when it's the pattern he likes and is presented realistically. And when hooked he fights with a determination few fish his size can surpass. Last but not least, when he's taken fresh from the icy water and cooked over a stream-side fire his flavor is out of this world. Devoted Brook Trout anglers even refuse to fry the fish in butter, claiming it detracts from the flavor. And in respect for their hero they never say they "catch" a Brook Trout —they say they "kill" a Brook Trout because it sounds more honorable, like killing an elephant or tiger.

The original range of the Brook Trout was Northeastern North America from Labrador south to Virginia and west to the Mississippi, but he has been such a favorite that he has been stocked in most popular angling regions in the Western states and Western Canada. Probably no fish is subjected to greater fishing pressure. Most of the thousands of hatcheries in this country and Canada are concerned exclusively with producing Brook Trout and his relatives, the Rainbow and Brown Trout, to replenish the tons anglers take every year. As a result, most of those you "kill" are stocked hatchery fish. Only in wilderness waters can "wild" fish still be found. But both perform equally well on your fly rod and you can't tell the difference until you clean them. White flesh means a hatchery-reared Trout; a "wild" Trout's flesh is pink like Salmon. Recently, however, biologists have discovered that ocean shrimp added to the diet of a pool-reared fish will turn its flesh pink, also, and so soon there'll be no way of telling the difference.

Technically the Brook Trout is a "charr" rather than a true Trout, but this needn't concern the angler because the differences are slight, such as the arrangement of teeth, and a tail that is square instead of forked. He is a pretty fish but not gaudy, a dark olive-green with an overlay of wavy dark markings along his back and a sprinkling of prominent red and white spots on his sides. His belly varies from pink to deep red, and the front edges of his fins are trimmed a pure white.

BROOK TROUT

RAINBOW TROUT

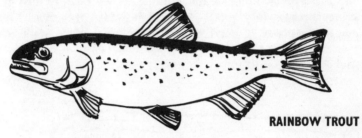

BROWN TROUT

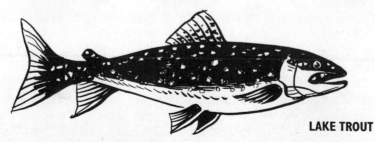

LAKE TROUT

27

His size, varying according to the size of the water and the amount of food available to him, ranges from $\frac{1}{2}$ to 5 pounds. His world record is $14\frac{1}{2}$ pounds. His diet depends upon his size. Brook Trout up to one pound feed almost exclusively on flies, and so these fish are the fly fisherman's ideal. Of course they also like earthworms, but the fly fisherman closes his eyes to this fact because he scorns bait-fishing for this aristocratic fish. Over one pound, the Brook Trout will still feed on flies but he doesn't find them very filling. He'd rather have a few plump minnows or crawfish.

In lakes, Brook Trout are found in the deepest holes formed by cold springs because they prefer the coldest water; they rarely survive temperatures over 70 degrees. In streams, when they aren't actively

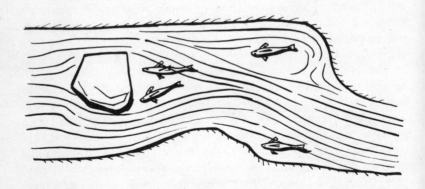

feeding you can find them resting in the swirls behind large submerged rocks, or in the quiet water at the edges of rapids, or in the deep pools. When hungry, they swim into the shallower water of the riffles below the rapids to feed on the late afternoon fly hatch.

A bitter truth to dry-fly fishermen is that spin-casting will take larger Brook Trout than will fly-casting, simply because the "lunker" Brookies prefer minnows, which the spinning lures imitate. Therefore these lures, fished deep over the spring holes, are best for lake fishing. A light rod (4 to 5 ounces) and 6-pound-test monofilament line (because it's practically invisible to the wary Brookie) are recommended. Change lures often until you find the type the Trout prefer. Often a fishing guide can suggest a pattern that is a consistent fish-getter for certain waters.

But no sport can top fly-fishing for the smaller Brook Trout in a tumbling stream. Use a 3- to 4-ounce fly rod, a torpedo-tapered line (for distance in casting), and a 9-foot leader tapering to 4X for dry flies, or a 6-foot leader tapering to 2X for wet flies. Use the wet flies when no Trout are breaking the surface, and use dry flies when the Trout are rising to a fly hatch. In that case use a pattern that matches the hatching flies as exactly as possible. For a choice of wet flies, it's wise to use the pattern that local fishermen tell you is best for the particular stream, and if it doesn't produce, experiment with other patterns.

For fishing wet or dry flies, you'll need boots or waders. Wade and cast upstream as you fish so you'll be out of sight to Trout that are above you, facing the current, and also so that any silt your feet dislodge will be carried downstream away from the Trout, not toward them to alarm them. Cast your fly beyond your target so it will drift submerged, or float, over the likely spot, and retrieve the slack line quickly so you'll be able to strike immediately when the Trout hits. If you delay an instant, he'll spit out the fly. In deep, wide streams cast above and across the current to drift the fly downstream past you. Be ready for a hit when your line tightens and swings the fly around below you.

There are many tricks to fool stream Brook Trout when conventional methods fail. Sometimes they won't take your flies simply because they're resting and are too lazy to move. Then the remedy is to stir them up. Get them excited! The simple way to do this is to take a large handful of pebbles and toss it into the stream, then cast your fly on top of the splash. Crazy? Not very! The sound will attract their attention and frequently they'll think it was caused by other fish feeding, especially if they're hatchery-reared Trout because in their hatchery they were fed in just that manner—by handfuls of food splashed into the water. And not wanting to miss their share, they'll usually swim out to grab your fly just in the spirit of competition, before another Trout gets it. This trick will work only once in the same spot, however.

There's even a trick for the garden-hackle dunker—the worm fisherman. Bait your hook with a lively worm, pinch a light split-shot

about 6 feet up your leader, and let your line drift downstream until the sinker catches under a rock and stops the drift. Then sit back on the bank and wait! The worm will swing enticingly back and forth with the current while the sinker holds it. It won't be long before a Trout sees it and finds it too tempting to resist. When you jerk the line to set the hook, the sinker will pull free from the rock.

RAINBOW TROUT

The honor of being one of the most spectacular fresh-water fighters must go to the Rainbow Trout. He takes a dry fly, or wet fly, or spinning lure without showing as much discrimination as do the Brook Trout and Brown Trout but during the ensuing battle he's out of water as often as he's in it, each time exploding into the air like a submarine missile. And at the end of these violent acrobatics you're often left with nothing but a rod with a snapped leader. The Rainbow is also distinguished for being one of the largest Trout. His world record is an amazing 37 pounds! And in addition, when his lake or river connects with the sea he frequently becomes "anadromous," taking trips to salt water and returning to fresh water to spawn. In this case he's called a Steelhead Trout.

The original waters of the Rainbow Trout were those of the West Coast from California to Southern Alaska, but he has been transplanted all over the world. One reason has been that he's an easy species to breed and rear in a hatchery. Another is that his eggs, if kept moist, will stay alive for months, even without refrigeration. And he makes himself at home in almost any lake, river or stream as long as its temperature doesn't climb above 70 degrees and as long as there's enough food to satisfy his voracious appetite. In spite of his record size, his average weight is 2 pounds. The giant specimens are found in Lake Pend Oreille, Idaho, as was the 37-pounder, and for years it was thought that these were a different species of fish. But finally it was discovered that their great size was due to the lake's huge horde of small Blueback Salmon upon which they fed. In general, the larger the water, the larger the Rainbow Trout. But from the angler's viewpoint, there's an objection to the monster Rainbows: the larger they are the lazier they are—the less they fight and the less they jump. And a Rainbow's jumps are half the thrill of catching him.

The Rainbow Trout is a true Trout with a forked tail, unlike the Brook Trout which is classified as a "charr." His back and upper sides are an olive-blue fading to a bluish-silver on the belly, and except for his belly he is covered with numerous small black spots. But his most outstanding coloration, which inspired his name, is a broad pink band extending along his sides from gill covers to tail. In older male Rainbows living in the dark depths, this pink frequently deepens to a brilliant and startling crimson. As a Steelhead, the seagoing Rainbow has the same coloring but the salt water has a fading effect. His back lightens to a pale blue and his sides become silver, the black spots almost disappear and he has only a suggestion of a pink band. But he regains his former brilliance some time after his re-entry into fresh water.

The Rainbow Trout's diet depends on his size. Up to one pound he gorges himself on insects and flies, but the heavier fish look for more substantial food, chiefly other fish. He is a wanderer, even when landlocked in fresh water. In a lake he may be roaming anywhere in search of food. Here the accepted method of taking him is trolling from a boat with a stiff bait-casting rod, a line of 10-pound-test (stronger if the lake contains heavy fish), and a large silver spoon or wobbling Bass plug. Lures must be weighted so they'll run deep. In the great depths of Pend Oreille, metal lines sometimes are used to carry the lures to the bottom, but all this extra weight limits the Trout's ability to fight.

In a stream the Rainbow likes the swiftest water, particularly the boil at the bottom of a falls, the riffles and the fast water that rushes beneath an overhanging bank. But if you miss a good fish at one of these spots, you won't find him there tomorrow because he's a wanderer even in a stream. Usually it's spring or summer when you meet him, and then he's traveling downstream after his winter spawning in the stream's headwaters. In late fall he starts back up again. Why the downstream migration? Maybe he's instinctively seeking the sea, as some biologists think all Rainbows do, not only the Steelhead. In large streams and rivers, spinning lures are deadly for Rainbow Trout, more so than for Brook or Brown Trout because of the Rainbow's extra fondness for minnow-like lures, but fly tackle always provides the most sport even when it doesn't take the most fish. Use the same rod, line, leader and flies recommended for Brook Trout, and also the same methods. Of course, when heavier fish are around, a heavier leader is advisable. And there's an addition. Since the Rainbow Trout prefers minnows, he's especially susceptible to flies that resemble these bait-fish—the streamer flies. Choose a streamer pattern such as a Grey Ghost or Green Ghost or a Nine-Three, and cast it up and across the stream, letting the current carry it down and below you. But as it drifts, retrieve it in short, snappy jerks so it resembles a darting minnow. If there's a

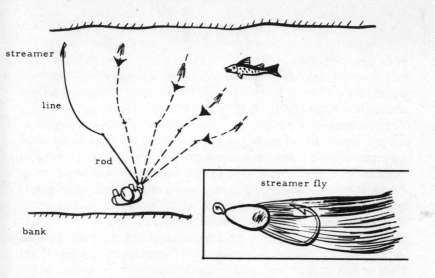

streamer

line

rod

bank

streamer fly

Rainbow within range and he's at all hungry, it will be hard for him to pass it up.

Sometimes a big stubborn Rainbow is as much of a bully as a big Bass—and just as easy to anger. There's a way to rile him up and make him biting mad. Always carry a couple of huge, gaudy Bass-type flies in your tackle, and when a Rainbow ignores your perfect imitation Trout fly you offer him so skillfully, insult him! Tie on one of the monstrosities, toss it across the stream and drag it in so fast it skitters over the surface, leaving a wake behind it. What he thinks it is is a mystery, but 9 times out of 10 he'll smash it!

BROWN TROUT

If there's a fish that deserves more appreciation from American anglers, it's the Brown Trout. He's highly respected in England, where angling first became an art. This Trout is larger than either the Brook Trout or Rainbow Trout; the world record Brownie, taken in Scotland, scaled 39½ pounds, and even in our large streams and lakes 8-pounders are common. He can survive in murkier and warmer waters (80 degrees) than can other Trout, and if it weren't for him there would be no Trout fishing at all in many of our warm southern streams and in many northern streams which have become partially muddied and polluted as civilization has deforested the wilderness areas.

Moreover, no fish offers a greater challenge to the fly angler. The Brown Trout is the most discriminating varmint you'll meet. Even when he likes your fly, it may take him 15 minutes to make up his mind to go for it. And then he may snatch it so viciously that your leader snaps before you realize what has happened. Or he may mouth it so gently that if you aren't wise to his ways he'll spit it out before you can hook him. He's frequently criticized as being a sluggish fighter, which is true in warm streams, but in the cold Brook Trout and Rainbow Trout waters he's guaranteed to smash your tackle faster than any other Trout his size. He's amazingly powerful, putting on a running, head-wagging battle that makes you think you're fast to a runaway torpedo. He doesn't leap like a Rainbow, but neither does a Brook Trout. The only really legitimate criticism of him is that his softer flesh often tastes more like panfish than Trout.

Our Brown Trout is a naturalized citizen, first transplanted in this country in 1803, and you can find him everywhere except in the extreme Southern states and Canada. Germany was his original home and sometimes he's still called German Trout. He's also called Loch Leven Trout, a name he received in Scotland, which was one of the first countries to adopt him. In color he's a dark brown tinged with olive on his back and upper sides, shading to a lighter olive-brown toward the belly. His back is covered with dark brown or black spots, his sides with bright red spots each encircled by a white ring. Old males develop a hooked jaw which gives them a pugnacious look.

The Brown Trout is not a wanderer; in searching for food he doesn't forsake his chosen home which in a lake or river is most frequently some large underwater obstruction (on which he can snag your leader when you hook him) or a deep flow beneath an overhanging bank. In a stream he likes to lurk in front of the large boulders that break the current, seldom behind them as do other stream Trout. You'll also find him at the lower ends of the deep pools. Brown Trout are present in most Rainbow Trout waters although you might not know it because an eager Rainbow will almost always get to your fly first. For dinner fare the Brownie likes insects and flies, even when he grows to monster size, but to fill his belly he must supplement these with worms, frogs, snails, minnows and anything else edible that comes his way, such as a stray field mouse.

During the day a Brown Trout in a lake or river can be persuaded to take a minnow-like spinning lure retrieved at moderate speed past his lair. But don't give up if the first few casts fail to bring results. Cast a dozen times, using a different lure each time. Use a stiff spinning rod with thin but strong (8-pound-test) monofilament line; a heavy line will scare him off more quickly than anything else. For fly fishing in a lake or river, fish from a boat and work the shore beneath the over-hanging bushes in early morning and late evening when he comes into shallow water looking for flies. Make no noise with the oars and never use a motor. He prefers dry flies to wet ones. When you cast the dry fly toward shore, let it rest on the surface at least 15 minutes before you pick it up for another cast. Twitch it but don't jerk it; if it moves so as to leave a wake on the surface he surely won't touch it. Use a standard dry-fly Trout rod with a 9-foot or 12-foot leader tapered to 4X. He might snap the light 4X tippet but he's apt to see a heavier one and not strike at all. In fly patterns he usually likes the less colorful ones such as a Black Gnat or the brown variations. Use the same fly tackle when stream fishing for Brown Trout, and the same techniques as described for Brook Trout—but be a hundred times more careful.

A Brown Trout is one of the most difficult fish to fool but it can be done, and here's one way to do it repeatedly although it requires some casting skill. When casting your dry fly toward shore at dawn or dusk, don't cast to drop the fly on the water; cast it further so it lands on a low overhanging bush. Then twitch the tip of your rod several times. The fly will loosen and drop lightly on the water. What could be more realistic? If your fly refuses to become unsnagged from the bush, pull

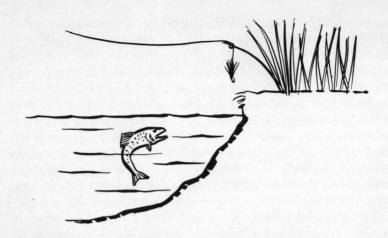

your line hard to break it off, tie on another fly and try again. So what, if you lose a few flies! This trick will get you a nice Brownie—and a few lost 25 cent flies are a cheap enough price to pay for him.

LAKE TROUT

The Lake Trout has several qualities that make him a fish you'll like to catch. First is his size. A 5-pounder is an infant; 20-pounders are common. The world record Laker taken on hook-and-line was 63 pounds, 2 ounces, and almost 4 feet long. Specimens weighing over 100 pounds have been netted by commercial fishermen. Second is his tremendous appetite that usually prompts him to gobble just about anything that comes his way, including your lures, as long as they look reasonably edible. Third is the fact that he's no weakling. As you might expect, he's a heavyweight slugger who hits hard enough to tear the rod out of your hands, and then he takes off, daring you to try to hold him. Finally, when you take him from the frying pan or oven, he's a feast for a king—usually enough for a dozen kings.

Because the Lake Trout is a "charr," not a true Trout, his closest relative is the Brook Trout. And he likes water that's even colder than does the Brookie—40 to 50 degrees. Therefore you'll seldom find him in water south of the Great Lakes. He's numerous in Alaska and Canada, where he's referred to as the Mackinaw Trout, and he's a favorite in Maine where they call him by the Indian name "togue." The Canadian Indians called him "namaycush" which means "dweller of the deep," a name that fits him exactly because he's rarely found in lakes less than 40 feet deep. He prefers them much deeper; in some waters you'll have to fish 800 feet down to reach him! And then when you finally haul him to the surface after he's given up the fight, his mouth will be open and his gills spread wide. He has died from a condition similar to the "bends" which endangers the lives of deep-sea divers when they ascend to the surface too quickly.

The color of the Lake Trout is primarily gray, the shade darkening with the fish's age and depth of water and sometimes taking on an olive cast. His deep-bellied body is covered with small light spots and in large fish the jaws become hooked, giving them a vicious appearance. The Lake Trout's diet consists mainly of other fish, especially fresh-water Smelt, without which it is doubtful that many Lakers would survive. Every Lake Trout water has been found to contain hordes of these small silver fish. And because of them, once a year the Lake Trout will provide you with excellent fly fishing—immediately after the ice leaves the lakes in the early spring. It is then that the Smelt crowd into the mouths of the streams to spawn and the smaller Lake Trout (up to 10 or 15 pounds) follow them into this shallow water to feed on them. Then the Lakers can be taken on fly tackle: a heavy glass (because it's more durable than bamboo) fly rod of 6 ounces or more, a 10-pound-test untapered leader, and a large streamer fly that resembles a Smelt, such as a Grey Ghost. But the accepted method of using this fly tackle is trolling, not casting. Troll your streamer on the surface along the shoreline on about 100 feet of fishline behind an outboard motor.

This fishing lasts only a few weeks; then the Smelt return to deep water with the Lake Trout chasing them. But there's one more period when you can take Lake Trout on flies: in the late fall when they come to the mouths of the streams to do their own spawning. And at this time you're more likely to snag a monster because they all make the trip. The same streamer-trolling method is best.

The majority of Lake Trout, however, are taken by trolling during spring and summer with large silver spoons or strings of large spinners. These are trolled behind a motorboat through the deepest holes in the lake. Ask the local guides, fishermen or game warden where these holes are, and when you have chosen one to try, test its depth with a sinker tied to your line. You'll have to fish your spoon down to within 10 feet of the bottom, so troll with a heavy nylon line (at least 25-pound-test) weighted with heavy sinkers tied above the lure. For very deep water

you'll need a line made of monel metal or copper wire to sink the lure deep enough. A short stiff glass rod and a surf-casting type of reel will handle the nylon line with its sinkers for semi-deep trolling. For the metal line you'll need a special windlass-type reel and a special 2-foot-long rod that's mostly handle and reel-seat. Once you've gotten a fish, keep trolling over the same spot and the chances are you'll pick up another on each pass because Lakers frequently remain in schools.

The Indians, using lures made of shells, had a method of catching Lakers when they weren't biting and it still works for anglers who are familiar with it. Anchor your boat directly over the deep Trout hole, put a slice of panfish on the hook of your spoon and lower the lure until it rests on the bottom. Let it rest a few seconds, then raise it a few feet with a hard, fast jerk. Let it settle back, jerk it up again and repeat. On one of these jerks you'll feel a fish. Why? Your fluttering lure attracts the school of Lake Trout and they cluster over it, sniffing it in curiosity. One of them eventually might grab it. Even if he doesn't, it won't be long before one will get in the way of the hook when you jerk it upward—and you'll have Lake Trout for dinner!

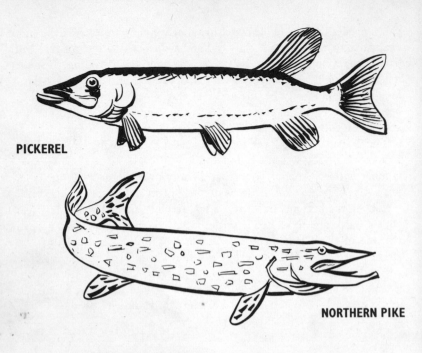

PICKEREL

NORTHERN PIKE

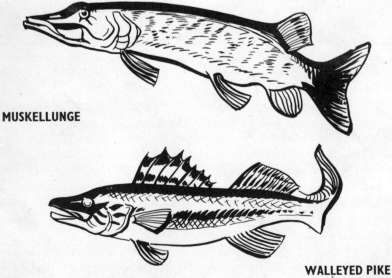

MUSKELLUNGE

WALLEYED PIKE

PICKEREL

The Pickerel is the smallest member of the Pike family, which includes the Northern Pike and Muskellunge, but he's no featherweight fighter. His average is 2 pounds and his world record is 9 pounds, 3 ounces. And he's savage enough for a fish many times his size. He isn't discouraged because his mouth, rimmed with fine teeth, is too small for him to swallow a fat Perch, Sunfish or Shiner at a single gulp the way a Black Bass can. When he pounces on a prey he seizes it across its middle, then shakes it like a terrier shakes a rat. When it's dead or too crippled to escape, he releases it, carefully turns it around to streamline it so it will fit his mouth, then slides it down his gullet headfirst. He's fast enough to catch any prey, too—long and slender with his swimming fins at the rear of his body, built for sprinting. One moment you'll see him staring at you malevolently from beneath a nearby lily pad, the next moment he's mysteriously disappeared. He doesn't swim off like other fish; he just seems to vanish. And he doesn't leave right away. Sometimes he'll let you touch him with an oar. He's not scared of you or anything else!

Once I hooked a small panfish on a fly and while I was playing it, it suddenly started to fight like a heavyweight. In amazement, I fought it for several minutes. When I finally reeled it in close, I saw a Pickerel had hold of it. He hadn't grabbed the hook, which was in the panfish's mouth, but had clamped his jaws across the fish's belly. When he saw me he let go and swam away—laughing, if a fish can laugh!

The Pickerel is found throughout the eastern United States from Maine to Florida and west to the Mississippi. He has a long, tubular body and a flat mouth shaped somewhat like an alligator's. His color varies greatly. When he has a chain-like pattern of dark lines on his sides he's called a Chain Pickerel. On a Grass Pickerel these dark lines are wavy. They become curved bars on a Barred Pickerel. In general, however, he's dark green on back and sides with a yellowish belly. In waters with a large iron content his sides and belly become a beautiful greenish-gold.

The Pickerel will be content with slow-moving rivers and streams, but his favorite waters are quiet lakes and ponds where he hides in the shallow weed beds or in the lily pads that fill the small coves. He's strictly carnivorous. Seldom will he touch flies or worms. He dines on other fish, mostly panfish, and frogs and stray field mice when he can get them. A live Shiner (type of minnow), with your hook placed lightly under the skin of its back so it will remain lively, will tempt him every time. Anchor your boat over an offshore weed bed or just outside the lily pads and let the Shiner swim off with your hook and line. But when a Pickerel grabs the bait and your line starts to run out, let him go. Don't try to hook him—yet. Remember the Pickerel seizes his food sideways. Wait until the line stops. Then the Pickerel is releasing the Shiner and turning it around to swallow it headfirst. When the line starts moving again, that's the time to strike him. Should you miss him by striking too soon, put on another Shiner and try again—he doesn't get discouraged easily.

You'll get the greatest thrill, however, by catching Pickerel on surface lures. They'll smash a surface lure so viciously it'll scare you. Use a bait-casting rod, an 8-pound-test line, and a reliably weedless lure such as a single-hook silver spoon. Put a strip of prepared pork rind on the hook and cast right into the pads, then retrieve fast so the lure skitters noisily over the tops of them. You'll see the pads scatter as the Pickerel homes in on your lure like a guided missile from his hiding place as far as 50 feet away, leaving a wake behind him. As soon as the lure drops into an open place among the pads, the water explodes and he's got it! Then you must work him around the pads so he doesn't get tangled in their stems. Casting non-weedless surface plugs—such as imitation mice, frogs and crippled minnows—into open pockets in the pads and at the edges of the pads and over deeper weed beds will take Pickerel, also, but not as often.

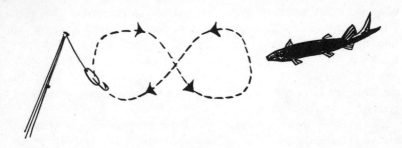

The Pickerel has one bad habit, however—he's a notorious lure-follower like the Pike and Muskellunge, especially in open water. When he isn't hungry, or he's suspicious, he will follow your lure right to the boat, his snout bumping the end of it, only to turn and swim off when you lift the lure from the water. And he'll repeat this on each successive cast until you're completely exasperated. But there are ways to fool him. When you see him coming in behind your lure, reel it to within 2 feet of your rod tip, then stick the tip deep into the water and move it so the lure swims in loops like a figure 8. This usually surprises him into striking. If it doesn't, on your next cast simply lift the lure from the water and dangle it in the air over his nose. But with either of these methods, be ready for him! If you don't give him line quickly when he strikes, he'll snap your rod like a matchstick.

NORTHERN PIKE

The most belligerent and fearless of all our fresh-water game fish is the Northern Pike. And the hungriest! He devours the equivalent of one-fifth his weight every day. And he is one of the few fish in the world that stalks his prey like an animal. His smaller cousin, the Pickerel, attacks immediately when hungry; the Northern Pike approaches cautiously, hiding from view in the weeds or bottom grass. Then when his victim is the least suspicious of danger and completely off-guard, he lunges. His prey usually is another fish such as a fat Yellow Perch, although it may even be a duckling or big bullfrog. He seizes it across its middle, cripples it, then turns it around to swallow it headfirst, as does the Pickerel. His pointed jaws, armed with long teeth, can easily hold his victim until it's helpless, no matter how much it may struggle. And Nature is his dentist; whenever he loses a tooth, she grows him another to take its place.

The Northern Pike is the middleweight fighter of the Pike family. He weighs in at about 4 or 5 pounds on the average but sometimes reaches 15 pounds. His world record stands at 46 pounds, 2 ounces although one caught in Germany unofficially weighed over 100 pounds! When hooked he engages in a slow but powerful and stubborn underwater battle. And he likes to "play 'possum," to make you believe he's surrendering so he can take you unawares—you reel him alongside the boat, get ready to gaff him (never net him because he's too big and vicious for any net to hold), and just at that moment he rockets into the air to throw the lure or break your rod with a snap of his head. He is long and slender like a Pickerel, but his olive-green back and sides are covered with unmistakable light yellow spots. In addition, his cheeks are fully scaled but his gill covers are scaled only on their upper halves. This distinguishes him definitely from the Pickerel, whose cheeks and gill covers are completely scaled, and from the Muskellunge, whose cheeks and gill covers have no scales below the level of his eyes.

Besides living on this continent from our Northern states north to Hudson Bay and Alaska, the Northern Pike is plentiful throughout Northern Asia and Europe (except Spain and Portugal). He likes large lakes which give him plenty of room to forage and which have the quiet waters most suitable to his stealthy characteristics. And he's a "lone

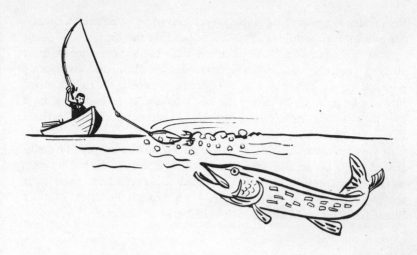

wolf," always living and hunting alone. From dawn until your breakfasttime you'll find him stalking in the offshore reeds and lily pads where he'll be after panfish. Here you can take him on bait-casting tackle, the same stout stiff rod recommended for Pickerel, but you'd better use stronger line—about 25-pound-test—and the rod should be glass to withstand the extra strain he'll exert on it. Also, use a 12-inch piano-wire or braided-wire leader between your lure and line to guard against his sharp teeth. Re-tie your line to it frequently because continued casting with a leader will soon fray the line where they join. For a lure, use a large weedless silver spoon, with a pork rind strip on its hook. Cast it directly into the pads and watch for a strike as soon as it reaches open water on the retrieve.

Still-fishing with live bait such as a 10-inch Yellow Perch or Sucker, hooked lightly beneath the dorsal fin and allowed to swim near the reeds or pads, is a sure thing for Northerns. Fish the bait as recommended for Pickerel. It is also effective in another haunt of the Northern Pike—the deep holes off the mouths of streams, island channels and the narrow entrances of bays, where Northerns lurk to ambush smaller fish who use these waterways. Here you can also take him by casting with a large, heavy wobbling spoon about 3½ inches long, colored red and white, or a silver spoon with a red-bucktail treble hook behind it.

Red, which suggests blood and injury, seems to be an especially appealing lure color to members of the voracious Pike family.

Northern Pike, like Pickerel, often will follow your lure without striking it and they usually can be persuaded the same way—by sticking your rod tip into the water near your boat and moving the tightly reeled lure in a figure 8. Or by lifting the lure from the water and dangling it over the reluctant critter's nose. But there's another teaser that Northern Pike seem to find irresistible, a sure cure for the "following" habit. Cast your spoon to the edge, or into a pocket, of the lily pads or reeds. Just as it hits the surface, reel in the slack line and lift the rod tip high so the spoon literally boils on the surface for several feet. Then lower the rod so the spoon slowly flutters down through the water. It won't flutter far! And you'd better have a tight grip on that rod!

MUSKELLUNGE

There are 40 different ways to spell the name of this fresh-water champion. Muskellunge is the most commonly accepted but the Algonquin Indians had the first. They called him "maskinonge," which means "great Pike." And no description could be more fitting. The Muskie is a Pike of a super variety. He's the meanest, most arrogant and one of the most difficult to catch of all fresh-water fish. He's also North America's most prized game-fish trophy. He's not scary like a Brown Trout. You'll see him take your live bait gently with his lips and hold it for a half-hour or more while you get a nervous breakdown waiting for him to make up his mind. He usually drops it, if you don't panic first and pull it away from him. Then he swims off scornfully. He'll follow your artificial lures without striking them not only time after time, but season after season. And he's even more a lone wolf than a Northern Pike. He'll live in the same lair for years until he's caught, then another Muskie moves in to take over his realm, which averages as much as a square mile of water. An angler sometimes goes after the same Muskie every year only to see his dream fish following every lure he casts. He prays that some day the monster will strike, and occasionally it happens. Then he's apt to get more than he expected. Many a hook-angered Muskie has charged the boat, leaping right over it—sometimes in it! Then it's like having a tiger by the tail and not being able to let go.

The Muskellunge is an all-American fish, ranging from New York State west to Minnesota and north through the Canadian provinces of Ontario and Quebec. His average weight is between 15 and 25 pounds; the world record taken on fishing tackle was 69 pounds, 15 ounces and over 5 feet long! Muskies are carnivorous from birth and young ones grow amazingly fast. In Muskie hatcheries, at 2 months they're about 6 inches long and each must be fed between 10 and 15 live minnows daily—they won't touch dead ones. In shape the Muskellunge is similar to the Pickerel and Pike but he has an underslung pot-belly bulging with food. His color varies from dark olive-green to dark gray with irregular black markings on his back, sides and fins. His positive identification are his gill covers and cheeks which have scales only on their upper halves. These are completely scaled on the Pickerel; on a Pike the scales are missing on the lower portions of the gill covers.

Muskellunge live only in very large lakes and their connecting rivers because they must have plenty of room not only for their own tremendous bodies but also to support the smaller fish on which they feed. A Muskie lair might be a sunken tree, a rocky hole near a bar off a jutting point of land, or a thick weed bed, all preferably in the deepest water. He leaves it to spawn in spring, and thereafter only to attack passing panfish, small animals that swim, ducks and other Muskies that come looking for a lair of their own. But too often he's able to tell the difference between natural food and one with an angler's hook fastened to it.

Casting over a Muskie hole is one way to tempt him. Try a selection of large 4-inch spoons with bucktail treble hooks of various colors, and retrieve them at various speeds and depths. Sharpen your hooks because a Muskie's jaws are tough gristle, and use a 12-inch wire leader on the lure for protection against his sharp teeth. A 30-pound-test line is advisable, and an extra strong glass casting rod—very stiff so you'll be able to sink the hooks in his tough jaw. Jerk the rod three or four times after he's taken the lure, to make sure he's solidly hooked. There are big plugs, too, which might fool a Muskie for you. One is designed to resemble a swimming baby duck. Another is supposed to imitate a swimming chipmunk.

It's possible to fly-cast for Muskies with heavy fly rods and large Bass-type flies, but only a few are taken on this tackle. More are taken by deep-trolling a large spinner-and-bucktail combination behind an outboard motor over all the known Muskie lairs, the theory being to visit them all on the chance that one fish might be hungry enough to strike. The method that pays off most often is trolling a dead 12-inch Yellow Perch or Sucker tied to a 6/0 hook so that it spins slowly or wobbles. But even this isn't guaranteed. With Muskies especially, you just can't beat realism.

But bait-casting provides the most sport because at least you can see the Muskie following your lure. And follow it he will. He never seems to get discouraged. After your twentieth cast, he's still there, his big nose bumping the lure's tail. The tricks to fool Pickerel won't work with him, such as moving the lure in a figure 8 when it's in close, or dangling it in the air over his nose. And the noisy-lure trick for

Northern Pike leaves him cold. But there is a way to fool this smart aleck—not every time but often enough. Give your lure a more realistic touch. Science has proved that fish identify their food by smell as well as by sight and sound. So carry with you a small bottle of cod liver oil. Drape a large tuft of cotton over your lure's rear hook and soak this cotton in the cod liver oil before each cast. How often do you think a Muskie can follow this hors d'oeuvre, inhaling its delectable fragrance, before he loses his self-control? Even a dead Sucker or Perch or a slice of fish-belly can't beat cod liver oil—they don't smell strong enough!

WALLEYED PIKE

The Walleyed Pike, also called simply Walleye or Pike Perch, can't be rated among the classiest of fresh-water fighters, but as a game fish he won't disappoint you. When you tackle him, he lets you know you're in a scrap. He's no midget; he averages 4 to 5 pounds and his world record is 22 pounds, 4 ounces. Add the fact that he's a school fish (when he's feeding, catch one and you catch a dozen), and you have a combination of weight and number that's sure to keep you pleasantly busy.

He's certainly one of our most interesting fish. First, he's misnamed. The word "Walleyed" accurately describes his large, glassy, staring eyes, but he's not related to the Pike family. Only in color does he look like one of the Pikes. He's dark olive-green, his sides covered with mottled dark green and yellow markings which sometimes are arranged in vertical bars. In reality he's related to the Yellow Perch, and is easy to distinguish from a Pike. He has the Perch's slightly humped back with two separate dorsal (top) fins set in the center of it like a Perch, whereas the Pike has a single dorsal fin set back near his tail. And the Walleye's mouth is stubbier although it is armed with formidable teeth like a Pike.

Another interesting aspect is his unique method of cooperative feeding. A band of Walleyes will form a semicircle and herd a school of minnows into a shallow pocket near shore where they can't escape, then their captors will dart in and grab them—not with a mighty splashing as most fish do, but in silence, without causing more than a ripple on the surface. Although minnows are their main natural food, Walleyes like nothing better than big, juicy nightcrawlers. They're interested in artificial lures least of all.

The Walleye is native to Canada and the Northern United States east of the Rocky Mountains as far as New Jersey, but he has been transplanted to most other states except those in the deep South.

Only the clearest waters are chosen by Walleyes for their haunts. You'll rarely find them where the bottom is muddy. In rivers and streams they like the deep flows at the bends and the deep pools below the fast current. In lakes they prefer the deep holes off rocky ledges and bars. But in late spring you can find the Walleye spawning in the shallow water and here you can take him on a spinning rod with 10-pound-test line and a small flashing spinning lure. But tie a dead minnow or hook a nightcrawler behind the lure because he's not easily tempted by a bare imitation. And use a 6-inch wire leader so his teeth won't cut your line. Light bait-casting tackle can be used if you prefer it.

Starting in June, the Walleye moves to his deep-water retreat where he remains during the day, returning to the shallows only at night to herd his minnows and feed. In states where night fishing is permitted, this is the best time to catch him. Use small luminous plugs or luminous spinning lures cast toward shore and retrieved slowly. When you can't tackle him at night, the next best times are at dusk when he's approaching the shallows, and at dawn when he's leaving them. This is especially true on overcast days.

During daylight, anglers find that the Walleye in deep water won't pay much attention to a cast or trolled lure, even when there's a dead minnow or worm tied to it. His belly is so full from his feast of the previous night that he'll usually refuse even a live minnow, frog or squirming nightcrawler, although these are considered most likely to interest him at this time. But it won't hurt to try. Hook the minnow lightly under its dorsal fin so it can swim around near the bottom. When you use a frog, hook it through the upper lip or tie it in a special frog harness available at any tackle shop. Then anchor your boat, drop your bait to the bottom and settle down with a good book. And hope!

But these Walleyes have their weaknesses in spite of their full bellies, as old-time Walleye anglers have discovered. They take Walleyes by casting lures in deep water during the day. They weight the spinning lure so it reaches the bottom and then let it scrape along the sand,

pebbles or stones as they retrieve it after a cast. Suddenly a fish snatches it. Why? No one knows! Maybe the Walleyes are sleeping and the sound awakens them and one of them grabs the lure before he realizes what he's done. And these anglers have another "sound" trick for bait-fishing. They tie a sinker to the end of the line and tie the hook about a foot above it. A foot above this hook they add a silver spinner. For bait they use the largest, liveliest nightcrawler they can find, hooked once through the band around its center so it can squirm freely. Then they fish this rig by jigging it up and down on the bottom. The sinker makes a noise every time it hits; the flashing spinner shows the Walleye where the sound is coming from. The next thing he sees is that big nightcrawler—and hungry or not, he's hooked!

CATFISH

CARP

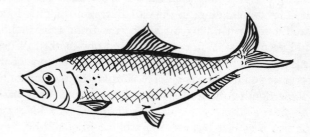

SHAD

CATFISH

Proof of the Catfish's popularity is the great number of anglers interested in him; they total several million. It is doubtful if even the aristocratic Trout, or the little Sunfish caught in nearly every back-yard pond, claims more attention than this strange fish with the whiskers. Maybe it's because there are more of him. The Catfish family contains over 1,000 species, distributed all over the world except in the coldest regions. In this country the Channel Catfish is favored by the sportsman because he's one of the largest and he's a tough fighter who will take a bait without too much coaxing. His home is the waters east of the Rocky Mountains from Canada to Mexico. South of Mexico you'll find his various cousins all the way to the southernmost tip of South America. A species in the Amazon—the Manguruyu—reaches several hundred pounds. Some varieties even take to salt water.

Our Channel Catfish averages 2 pounds in weight. His world record is 55 pounds. The Blue Catfish, or Mississippi Catfish, is larger but not as widespread, being confined to the Mississippi Valley. His world record is 94 pounds, 8 ounces. The Catfish has a firm, chunky body covered with smooth skin instead of scales. And sprouting from his chin are long and tough whiskers, called "barbels," which inspired his name since they give him a somewhat cat-like appearance. He uses them as a kind of radar to guide him in the dark during his nightly foraging. Be very careful when handling a Catfish; the front spines of his dorsal (top) and pectoral (side) fins are sharp and saw-toothed. When danger threatens he raises them and a stab in the hand from one of them isn't an experience you'll forget in a hurry. Fortunately they're not poisonous as on some South American species. The Channel Cat's back is dark gray, his sides a silvery gray, and he's sprinkled with black spots. The Blue Catfish is similar but more of a bluish-gray and he doesn't have spots. Both have deeply forked tails.

As for diet, it would be easier to list what a Catfish doesn't eat. He likes everything, even some things that seem impossible. He won't pass up any natural food such as flies, insects, minnows, frogs, worms, crawfish and the rest. And he has quite an appetite for new items introduced to him by anglers: chopped fish, chicken and hog livers, chicken entrails and coagulated chicken blood, rabbit, squirrel, beef, lamb and an assortment of ready-made commercial products accurately called "stink bait." The more it stinks, the more the Catfish seems to like it, probably because he can smell it at a greater distance. But in spite of his strange taste in foods, the Catfish likes a clean home. You'll find him generally in the pure, clean waters of lakes and fast rivers with sand or pebble bottoms. Only a few of his cousins are happy in muddy homes.

In these waters the Catfish varies his haunts and feeding habits, although he more frequently feeds on the bottom and at night. In spring in good Catfish water look for them in the warm shallow coves of ponds and lakes, and in the deep fast current of streams and rivers, where they roam feeding during the dusk, night and dawn. During the day they retreat to deep rocky shelters in a lake; to deep pools under overhanging banks and tree bottoms in a river. When the summer heat arrives, Catfish remain in the coldest waters, leaving them only at night to feed and during dark overcast and rainy days. Autumn offers some of the best Catfishing. Then they increase their activity and come into the shallows more often in search of insects as well as bottom food, and they become sport for the fly-fisherman. Use regular Trout tackle.

Although many Catfish are taken on flies and spinning lures, the most and largest always seem to be caught on bait. For this fishing, use a strong bait-casting rod stiff enough to sink your hook in a Cat's tough mouth, and a bait-casting reel with line of about 12-pound-test. Bait-

fishing at night, where legal, is done without a bobber. Let the bait (any of the tidbits listed above) rest on the bottom or roll with the current. When you are casting during the day and artificial lures won't produce results, try a frog, crawfish, minnow or a bunch of nightcrawlers strung on a plain hook. A spinner added a few feet above the hook will help attract the Cats. In clear water, use a 3-foot monofilament leader, too.

The "stink baits," although unpleasant to smell and handle, are nevertheless the most effective if you want to be *sure* of catching Catfish. You can concoct your own, such as "sponge bait"—made by cutting a sponge into small cubes and letting these soak in a jar of mixed limburger cheese and dead fish for several days, after which each cube is used as a single bait. But there's a simple and deadly Catfish bait that doesn't smell bad. An old Catfisherman passed it on to me. He had learned that Catfish like soap! His bait was a small chunk of white laundry soap into which he embedded his hook. When in the water, the soap gradually dissolved, sending out a trail of scent for the fish to follow, just as the "stink baits" do. He had a string of nice Cats to prove his invention worked! And since then, I've often proved it myself.

CARP

Anglers have mixed feelings about the Carp. Most of them don't like him, although he's fun to catch on the right tackle. And he's not bad to eat when he's skinned and the narrow band of pink flesh that runs along each of his sides is cut out before he's cooked. As a matter of fact, as a food item he tops all other fresh-water fish. Originally a native of Asia, and related to the common Goldfish, he has spread throughout the world and has become a major source of high-protein nourishment to people of every continent. In the United States alone an estimated 20 million pounds of Carp are marketed annually, although fish-eaters consider him too soft and bony to be a delicacy. The trouble with Carp from the angler's standpoint is that he chokes out other game fish. He not only competes with them for live food when he becomes large enough to grab it with his small mouth, but he spends most of his life as a vegetarian, digging up plants to nibble on their roots and thus destroying the vegetation which other fish need for refuge and spawning. And his digging stirs up the bottom mud and silt, making the water too dirty for cleaner species. His greatest sin is probably his habit of searching for and feeding on the roe (eggs) of other fish. The only way to get rid of him once he's become established in a lake or pond is to poison the water to kill all the fish. Then, when the water has again purified itself, it can be stocked with game fish.

Whenever you have a few minnows left over after a day of fishing, don't dump them into the lake! There might be some Carp among them and if so, you'll be planting the seeds that will eventually destroy all the lake's game species. You'll never be able to get rid of the Carp by catching them on fishing tackle. Even the commercial netters take only a small percentage. The reason is simply that the Carp is probably the most intelligent fish you'll ever meet! And the most difficult to deceive! Actually he is one of the greatest challenges to your ability as an angler.

In this country his weight averages between 2 and 5 pounds but 50-pounders occasionally are taken. His Asiatic cousin, the Mahseer, grows to 400 pounds. He is a solid, large-scaled fish with unusual teeth—they're in his throat. Growing from his small mouth on each side are two short whiskers, or "barbels." His color depends upon where he lives. In waters with sand, pebble or rocky bottoms he's usually a silvery-yellow, almost the color of brass. In muddy waters he turns various shades of green, brown or black.

In a river or lake that contains Carp, they're apt to be feeding anywhere. But since they aren't dummies, you'll have to make an extra effort if you expect to outwit them. Start by selecting a certain spot where you can see bottom, and "bait" this spot for a week or longer with chopped vegetables such as potatoes, carrots and turnips. Don't drop them on the water; they'll spread too far as they sink. Place them in a pail, lower the pail to the bottom, then up-end the pail to dump them in a space about one foot across. The Carp will find them. When you discover that your bait is disappearing, you'll know the Carp are visiting it, and that's the time to go fishing. But first observe from your quiet, anchored boat how cautious they are. A Carp will mouth a small piece of vegetable a dozen times, spitting it out quickly each time, before he makes up his mind to swallow it.

For tackle, use a strong glass fly rod and a 9-foot leader of thin monofilament. A heavy leader will make him shy away. Your hook must be small, about a No. 12 or smaller, and your best bait will be doughballs. Make these by taking heavy bread dough, or the center of fresh-baked bread, and rolling it into pellets the size of large peas. Mix thin fibers of absorbent cotton in with the dough so the pellets

won't dissolve quickly in the water. Also add some honey, sugar or anise oil for scent. Of course you can use bits of vegetable for bait, too, but Carp seem to be especially tempted by bread dough, and it is more durable and will stay on the hook longer.

Embed your small hook in a doughball so it's completely hidden and cast it close to your baited spot. Add a small split-shot sinker on the leader if the current tends to move the bait away. The slightest twitch of your line means a strike; jerk your rod immediately before the Carp rejects the dough. When he's hooked, lead him away carefully into shallow water so he won't disturb the other feeding fish. He'll come peacefully, as yet unaware that he's in trouble. But be ready when he reaches the shallows—that's when the fight starts. And a big Carp is as strong as a bulldozer. Fight him slowly, trying not to make a fuss that will alarm the others. If he swims back to his companions, move around and lead him off to the other side before putting rod-pressure on him again. With luck in keeping the peace, your homemade fishing hole will pay off with several more Carp in succession before you have to let it rest till another day.

SHAD

In one respect the Shad is a new fish—he's new to sport-anglers who only recently learned how to catch him on rod and reel. But he's an old friend of millions of Americans who have been dining on him and Shad roe ever since the Indian days. The fact is that until 1930 the only known way of taking Shad was by netting them. Then some enterprising anglers on New England's Connecticut River discovered a type of lure this fish would strike. In so doing they also discovered a slashing, leaping, frenzied fighter that ranks with the classiest of fresh-water fish.

The Shad can't accurately be termed a fresh-water species, however, because he's "anadromous," living most of his life in salt water and entering the rivers in spring to spawn. But it is only during these spawning runs into fresh water that the Shad can be caught by anglers, or netted. He's never been taken at sea; where he goes in the vast ocean is a complete mystery. Originally native to the Atlantic coast from Labrador to Florida, Shad have been transplanted to the Pacific coast and have become well established from Southern California to Southern Alaska. You won't mistake him for another species. He's a broad silver fish with a dark blue back and a half-dozen black spots on each side behind the gills. His tail is deeply forked, and the tip of his lower jaw has a slight hook which fits into a notch in his upper jaw. The males weigh from 2 to 6 pounds; the females, usually heavy with roe, average from 6 to 8 pounds. Netters have taken Shad as heavy as 13 pounds.

The difficulty in catching Shad on rod and reel has been that this fish doesn't feed during its spring spawning run into fresh water. A Shad makes the entire trip on energy he accumulated while feeding at sea. This is a precaution of Nature to prevent the Shad from eating his own spawn. And it is the problem that stumped the anglers for years—how can you get a fish to bite a hook when he isn't biting any-thing, even food? Anglers waded into river pools where big Shad were packed side by side like monster sardines, and offered them juicy nightcrawlers, fresh grasshoppers and minnows. For the first time these sure fish-getters failed. Artificial lures, from streamer flies to Bass plugs, were tried. All they did was send the Shad splashing in retreat. Then some angler in desperation used a red Trout fly, so old and beaten it was nothing more than a bare hook with a twist of tinsel and a wisp of feather. To add color, he threaded a red bead in front of it. A Shad rolled and snatched it—and history was made! Since then, several other

red beads   wrapped tinsel

a few red feathers

Shad fly

small Shad lures have been developed, but their number is limited and they must be fished in certain definite ways. Why do these non-biters bite them? Experts believe the Shad strike them instinctively, a reflex action from the days when they fed on small fish at sea.

A heavy glass fly rod is recommended when the water is low enough for you to wade within casting distance of the river pools where the Shad are resting during their runs; use spin-casting tackle when the rivers are so swollen that long casts are necessary, and also when there's no room behind you for a fly rod's backcast. Your fly should be a No. 4 or 6, and nothing more than a tinsel-wrapped hook with a single strand of feather—red for sunny days, yellow for dark days. Use 6 feet of 8-pound-test leader, but before tying your line to it, thread several small red beads on it and slide them down so they rest near the eye of the hook. Then pinch one or more split-shot sinkers to the leader to sink the fly close to the bottom. With a spinning rod, use the same setup. Or instead of the fly, try a small No. 0 silver spinner with a bare No. 4 hook behind it and the same red beads and leader ahead of it. Other

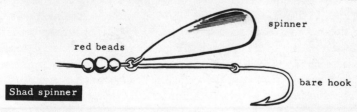

spinner

red beads

bare hook

Shad spinner

small spinning lures sometimes work in exceptionally rough water, but the Shad flies and the Shad spinner are the old faithfuls.

Shad fishing demands more patience than any other kind. It's not because you must wait for the fish to come. They're usually almost at your feet, flashing their bright silver sides at you every time they roll. Patience is needed because you won't get a strike a minute, or even every hour, in spite of the horde of fish. And it's difficult to keep your self-control when these monsters are so near that you can touch them. Moreover, once you've cast your lure you must leave it alone, like still-fishing. Repeated casting will only drive the Shad away. Let the current carry your fly or spinner into the nearest pool. When your line tightens, the lure should be about a foot from the bottom where the under-currents wave it enticingly under the Shads' noses. They won't touch it —not yet! They'll sniff it, bump it, roll over it, and finally swim away from it. But if you are patient, and stifle the impulse to reel in and cast again, eventually one of them will ease over and grab it! While you're hanging on to that ball of silver fire, you'll agree he was well worth waiting for.

Part 2—

Salt-Water Dock Fish and How to Fool Them

PORGY

Anglers along the east coast of the United States have the little Porgy to thank for much of their fishing fun. When this hungry denizen of the deep comes along he usually brings a few million of his brothers and the action is fast and furious. As soon as you pull one in, drop your hook and another will grab it. The commercial deep-sea netters account for the greatest haul; over 20 million pounds of Porgy reach the fish markets annually. This will give you some idea of the Porgy's value as a table delicacy. If you've never tasted one, you don't know what you're missing. And they taste even better when you catch them yourself and cook them fresh from the water.

The commonest Porgy of this country is called the Scup, and you'll find him in the Atlantic from Texas to Maine with the exception of Florida. But anglers of that state have Porgy, too, because he has many cousins. There you'll catch the Jolthead Porgy which ranges throughout the Caribbean south to Brazil, the Saucereye Porgy of the Florida Keys and Bermuda, and the Littlehead and Grass Porgies of the Keys and the West Indies. Other species, numbering 100 in all, are scattered throughout the world. The largest—the Musselcracker—is found off South Africa and reaches 100 pounds. Our Porgies run about a pound although a 2- to 4-pounder might occasionally surprise you. You can catch the Florida species all year 'round. Summer and fall are the best times for Scup.

The Porgy is oval and looks almost like a big fresh-water Sunfish because of his high forehead. His front teeth are "incisors," which means they have sharp edges designed for cutting. When feeding, he uses them to crack small crabs, squid, clams and mollusks which are the principal items on his menu. Although his tropical cousins are brilliantly colored with shades of blue, lavender, purple and gold, the Porgy that will most frequently reach your frying pan, the Scup, doesn't look quite as much like a rainbow. His back and sides are black or dark brown, his fins brown and his belly silver. But he's just as much sport to catch and even more delicious to eat.

The Porgy is classified as a "bottom" fish, which means he prefers to search the bottom for his food. During an incoming tide he follows the rising water into the shallow bays to feed. When the tide recedes, he follows it out again. To catch him, you must fish in the path of his in-and-out migrations with the tides. Your fishing spot may be a dock which extends into a deep channel, or a small boat anchored in the channel, or a bridge that spans it. Your tackle can be anything from a drop line, which is just a length of linen line with a hook and sinker, to an elaborate rod and reel. But if you want the most angling pleasure, use a light spinning or fly rod for these small fish and the fight they'll put up won't disappoint you. The only objection you might have to this tackle is that it won't let you pull them in as fast as a drop line would since you'll have to play them. Use small hooks, about No. 7, on short monofilament leaders or snells, and attach three of them to your line with a light pyramid-shaped sinker on the end. With spinning tackle, your line should be monofilament also. With fly tackle, use a short, level monofilament leader of at least 6-pound-test. Your rod should be the glass type which is less apt to be damaged by the salt water, but in any case wash everything thoroughly in fresh water—rod, reel, line and hooks—after each use.

Bait will catch more Porgies than artificial lures, but when these fish are feeding they'll take almost anything small enough to eat. Clams are excellent, as are crabs. Break the shells and place a small piece of meat on each hook, burying the hook completely in it if possible. Sandworms and bloodworms are probably the most widely used tempters for Porgy

64

PORGY

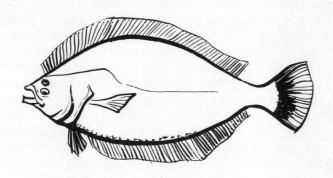

FLOUNDER

when they can be obtained. Almost all tackle stores near good fishing docks carry a supply of various baits. Since the Porgy is a bottom feeder, your bait should be on or near the bottom. The usual method is to cast out, let your rig lie still a few minutes, then reel it in for a short distance. The moving bait helps draw the fish if they are around.

As with most fishing, the first thing you have to do is find the fish. And the more territory you can cover with your bait, the better your chances of finding them. Therefore, in Porgy fishing especially, spin-casting has the advantage. It lets you cast your bait farther and in any direction, whether you're fishing from dock or boat. Artificial lures have some appeal for Porgies, although this species usually isn't crazy about them. But all fish are curious, and the Porgy is no exception. Use the lure as an attractor! For example: 3 feet above your baited hooks, insert a large spinner on your line, about a No. 5. Make several long casts, each time retrieving the spinner and baited hooks steadily, so the spinner revolves and flashes in the water. The next time, cast and retrieve only a short way—perhaps a dozen feet—then let the rig sink to the bottom. Wait several minutes before repeating. If any fish are around, not only Porgies, they'll come to look over the strange attraction. Your bait will do the rest. And don't be surprised if you snag something big, perhaps a Fluke or even a Striper, when your spinner is flashing while you're reeling in.

FLOUNDER AND FLUKE

The Flounder and Fluke belong to a family known as "flatfish" because they swim flat on their sides, horizontally, like swimming "doormats" as they are sometimes affectionately called. They're scrappy fighters and plentiful most of the year; you can catch Flounder off New England when it's so cold that icicles sprout from your fishing rod. They're a prized food delicacy, too. The "fillet of sole" you see on restaurant menus is usually our friend the Flounder. The true Sole, found only in Europe, and the Halibut are also members of the flatfish family which includes more than 500 species. The common Flounder of the Atlantic from Labrador to the Carolinas is technically called the Winter Flounder because he seems to enjoy icy waters. The larger Fluke, found from New England in summer to Texas, is technically the Summer Flounder. Along the Pacific Ocean from California to Alaska there's the Starry Flounder, so-called because he's covered with small star-shaped plates.

A baby flatfish starts life as a normal-looking fish—he swims upright, has an eye on each side of his head and a horizontal mouth below them. Then, as he grows, he undergoes an amazing transformation. One eye extends and moves down his face; the second eye gradually moves around his head to join the other eye on the same side; he flops over from a vertical to a horizontal swimming position—and he becomes a "flattie"—both eyes on top, a vertical mouth below them (horizontal before he turned on his side). His bottom side is bleached white and he's colored on the top side. What color? Practically any because the flatfish can change his color scheme like a chameleon to match his environment. He can match yellow and brown patterns very quickly. Greens and blues take several months. Only reds seem too much for him. This is part of Nature's plan of protective coloration, and the Flounder supplements it with a few tricks of his own. To hide, he swims close to the bottom and stirs up the sand or silt by rapidly vibrating the fins which almost entirely encircle his flat pancake body. Then he lies on the bottom and lets the sand and silt settle over him. Only his strange eyes remain visible. But as soon as an unsuspecting crab or shrimp happens by, the sand comes to life, the Flounder darts out to seize his meal, then returns to hide once more.

There's another startling fact about the flatfish. There are right-sided ones (with their eyes on their right sides) and left-sided ones (with eyes on their left sides). This is the way to tell the difference between a Flounder (Winter Flounder) and a Fluke (Summer Flounder); the former is right-sided, the Fluke is left-sided. The Starry Flounder can be either. The European Sole is right-sided, as is the largest of the flatfish, the Halibut, which in the Atlantic can reach 700 pounds. Imagine what a "flattie" that size could do to your tackle! But you're not likely to be bothered by such giants close to shore. The Flounder that furnishes food and fun for Atlantic inshore anglers is a nice panfish size—from $\frac{1}{2}$ to 1 pound. The Starry Flounder of the Pacific runs larger, from 2 to 5 pounds. The Atlantic Fluke is the largest of these three most popular angling species; he averages 5 pounds, with a world record of 20 pounds, 7 ounces.

Since the Flounder and Fluke are bottom feeders, hiding in the sand to pounce on their food, you must fish for them on the bottom, making your bait or its imitation move as naturally as possible. Sandworms, bloodworms, small shrimp, killies (minnows), strips of squid, pieces of clam or crab—all are on the flatfish's menu. For Flounder, use very small hooks because this species has a tiny mouth. Fluke have mouths large enough to take No. 1 hooks, but since they also have tooth-studded jaws, use heavy nylon leaders which they won't be able to chew through so easily. Any tackle from a drop line to rod-and-reel is suitable, although a light glass rod will furnish the most thrills, especially when a big Fluke runs off with your bait. Rig your line with a pyramid-type sinker at the end and three snelled hooks (hooks tied on short twisted nylon leaders, or snells) spaced above it about 2 feet apart. You can obtain your bait at any tackle store near the dock. Get an assortment of several kinds, then test a different one on each hook until you find which the fish are preferring. An incoming or high tide is best since the flatfish follow the current. Cast out as far as possible, let the baited hooks sink, then retrieve them in very slow jerks so they drag across the bottom in imitation of a crawling crab or grass shrimp or a feeding baitfish. If small fish or crabs steal your bait repeatedly, don't be discouraged! Throw a few handfuls into the water to make them happy. The more the merrier—and any feeding activity is sure to attract better and bigger fish.

Be sure to wash all tackle thoroughly in fresh water after use to get

rid of the highly corrosive salt. Spinning tackle is recommended for all dock and bay fishing because it will cast your bait farther and enable you to explore more water until you find the fish. But in Flounder and Fluke fishing it has a special advantage few anglers know about—strangely, these fish will take various spinning lures even when they refuse natural bait! When nobody around you is getting any action, break out a spinning rig and tie on it a small, weighted, yellow, red or white feathered streamer. Add a touch of bait to the hook for realistic scent. Cast the streamer, let it lie on the bottom a second, then twitch the rod while you reel in slowly, so the streamer hops along like an excited shrimp. A Flounder or Fluke in ambush will hit it harder than any you'll ever catch on bait!

SEA BASS

The Sea Bass is familiar to salt-water anglers of our Atlantic and Pacific Coasts—and, as a matter of fact, to anglers of almost every coast because his family of more than 400 species roams the tropical and temperate waters of the world. He grows the largest in the Gulf of Mexico and the Pacific where, known as the Giant Black Sea Bass, he's been netted at weights up to 1,000 pounds. Two of his family every angler will recognize are the Striped Bass and the White Perch. Along the Atlantic from Maine to Florida there is a variety known simply as Sea Bass—no giant, but a favorite of dock and inshore anglers. They like the greedy way he goes after a bait. The only thing they don't like about him is the place he chooses to call "home"—it's usually the rockiest hole in the ocean, just the spot for snagging hooks and lures and losing them. Whenever an angler hauls in one of these fighters, however, he seldom realizes what a fantastic little fish is flopping at the end of his line. This Sea Bass is one of the world's few creatures that can change its sex! It spends part of its life as a mother and part as a father. Researchers were amazed to learn that many Sea Bass function as egg-producing females until they are about 5 years of age, after which they become normally functioning males for the balance of their lives (about another 15 years).

The Sea Bass of the Atlantic is a chunky fish with large eyes and mouth, and is distinguished by a flat tail which is square on top and curved on bottom, a sort of half-round shape. He (or she) has a checked appearance due to a network of black lines across his back and sides, and this is emphasized by a white spot on each scale. His background color is usually a dark green-gray or blue-gray. Weight averages between one and 2 pounds; 4-pounders are rare. The world record is 8 pounds. The rod-and-reel record for the Giant Black Sea Bass in the Pacific is 514 pounds. For the Gulf of Mexico it's even larger: 551 pounds. But this fish also comes in not-so-giant sizes. A Pacific angler can spend many a busy afternoon pulling in the one-pound youngsters which feed in the shore waters. They show an interesting color difference, however. When fully grown the species is a dark brown-black with occasional light spots beneath chin and tail. But the angler's small Bass looks different enough to be another fish; its "baby" color is red with black spots!

SEA BASS

STRIPED BASS

WEAKFISH

Giant Sea Bass take no prizes for scrappiness on tackle. They're lumbering fighters that soon tire themselves by their own weight. But the small Bass of both coasts will put on a good show if you give him half a chance, which means catching him on a fly rod or light spinning rod. He's around from May till October but the hot days of July and August are best because then you'll find him feeding inshore. For the 2- to 3-pounders, you'll have to fish the deep rocky holes or a sunken wreck. And you might have to use a heavier rod, line and leader because the first thing a Sea Bass does when he feels the hook is streak for his lair, and if you can't stop him before he reaches it he'll break off among the snags. The smaller fish, however, come into the rocky shores, breakwaters, jetties and piers. They like to feed on the barnacles that cover the pilings. Half-pounders will gather by the thousands under a pier where fishing boats come in, waiting for the entrails of the day's catch when it is cleaned and tossed overboard. And here a fly-tackle angler can have as much sport as he can handle. Use a single small No. 1 hook on a 6-pound-test leader—not two hooks because two Sea Bass at one time are too much for fly tackle. Any bait will do. Even artificial flies will work when the Bass are in a feeding frenzy.

For the larger fish found off jetties and long, deserted docks and in deep rocky holes, Bass anglers consider bait the best taker. They use the meat of shrimp, crabs, clams or squid, and also sandworms or bloodworms. And they lose a lot of tackle when they fish for these bottom-feeding fish with a regular bottom-fishing rig, such as several hooks with a heavy sinker on the end, because the sinker often becomes wedged in the rocks. Usually they tie the sinker to the line with a weak leader so it will break free more easily, without taking the hooks with it, when it must be sacrificed. Sea Bass will take spinning lures, but the difficulty here is keeping the lure at the right depth—the top level of the rocks. If it's too high, the Bass won't touch it; too low, and you'll snag it among the rocks.

An almost sure thing for Sea Bass was shown to me some years ago and it hasn't failed me often. Tie a spinning lure (preferably one with red, white or yellow feathers) to the end of the line, and about 3 feet above it on 3 feet of weak leader tie a "dipsey" sinker (a shape least likely to snag). On the retrieve after casting, let this combination sink until you can feel the sinker bouncing across the rocks; the spinning lure then will be working at just the right distance above them. Should

the sinker snag, break it off by pulling the line hard; you still have your lure! Tie on another sinker. Cast carefully because sometimes the lure and sinker will tangle in the air during the cast, then on the retrieve the lure won't trail above and behind the sinker the way it should. Work this rig right and it'll get 'em every time!

STRIPED BASS

The Striped Bass, also known as just Striper or as Rockfish (south of New Jersey), has everything a game fish needs to be a champ—he's big, fights like a mad dog and hits your artificial lures with a wallop like few other salt-water fish. Also, he usually can be counted on for some unexpected trick that will leave you gasping—such as the Striper I once met (but didn't catch) that refused every lure cast to him and decided he wanted the one I'd left hanging over the side of the boat. He took it, along with the rod and reel it was tied to and the jacket that was lying across them. And then there was another Striper at a recent surf-casting tournament where the experts hadn't been able to catch any-thing over 22 pounds; he was caught by a small boy who was dunking a worm in the waves that washed the beach—and this Striper weighed 42 pounds!

Anglers on both coasts now can enjoy this species. The Atlantic was his native home until about 1880, when a few hundred infant fish were dumped into the water off California; now Pacific anglers catch as many as do those in the East—a total of several thousand tons each year! Sometimes it doesn't take as many Stripers to make a ton as you'd think. Their average weight is from 5 to 10 pounds but when the big "bull" Stripers are around, at 25 to 35 pounds apiece, the weight adds up fast. The world record on rod-and-reel was 5 feet long and weighed 73 pounds. The largest ever netted weighed over 125 pounds. There's another Striped Bass you might catch some day, smaller (average: 2 pounds) but just as full of fight. He's the fresh-water Striper! A number of years ago young salt-water Striped Bass were introduced into some southern fresh-water lakes and, miraculously, they not only survived but made themselves completely at home. You'll hear more about these fish as their popularity spreads. They look just like their salt-water ancestors except for being more colorful. The seacoast Striped Bass is generally a greenish- or brownish-black on back with silver or yellow-silver sides and a white belly. He gets his name from the 7 or 8 black stripes that line his sides from gills to tail and are his positive identification.

The Striper is a seasonal fish. The best periods for catching him are during spring and fall off the New England coast where Cuttyhunk

Island and Martha's Vineyard are the hottest fishing spots; in early spring and late fall along the East Coast from New Jersey to Florida; from June to January along the Gulf Coast; and from June to October along most of the West Coast. At these times you're likely to find him anywhere close to shore—under docks, bridges, along the banks of tidal rivers, in the channels, and in the surf. Try every fishy-looking spot, especially a "rip" (the line of churning water where two tides meet), and the channels at low tide, and the sand bars and flats at high tide. A dock projecting into a boat channel is a good fishing spot. Use spin-casting tackle with regular spinning lures, plus a strip of pork rind for more action, and a 10-pound-test line if the fish average less than 5 pounds where you're fishing. Heavier fish will require heavier line and tackle. Or use your spinning rod for long casts with bait such as squid, crab, grass shrimp, cut herring, a small eel or minnow, or a hookful of sandworms or bloodworms. Place a spinner in front of the bait and retrieve it slowly.

Always watch for signs of feeding Bass—explosions of white water in the same spot, noisy birds diving at baitfish the Stripers have driven to the top, and the swirls of big fish. Stripers feed at all depths and frequently you can see them chasing small minnows just below the surface. An old-timer once gave me his secret formula for catching Stripers: "Fish for them everywhere, with everything, and keep doing it!" He wasn't joking. A cruising band of Striped Bass might show up anywhere and at any time. A hundred casts off a corner of a dock might be in vain, and the next cast will snag one of them.

Casting fresh-water Bass plugs will take Stripers, too. Use your regular casting tackle but be sure to wash off all the salt with fresh water after using it so it won't corrode. Use large deep-running plugs and spoons when the water is rough, surface plugs when it's smooth. Special heavy-duty tackle is required to cast large Striped Bass lures long distances into the surf. If you have a boat and an outboard motor, trolling fresh-water or salt-water Bass lures frequently is as effective as casting them.

But the old-timer I mentioned previously liked still-fishing. It didn't work him as hard as casting. Besides, he had a still-fishing gimmick that seemed to catch everything, including Stripers. To his bait-casting line he'd fasten a snelled hook (one with a short snell or leader tied to it) of about 4/0 size, which would be large enough to discourage little fish.

A few inches above this he'd add a small sinker, and about 6 inches above the sinker he'd fasten a big red-and-white bobber, or float. Then he'd bait the big hook with all the grass shrimp, sandworms or crabmeat it would hold, sometimes with a whole crab, and he'd cast out from the dock to let this contraption ride along with the tide. And he'd keep jerking it constantly. This made the big red-and-white bobber hop and splash along the surface, and every time it hopped it jigged the bait up and down like a fish that was trying to reach the bobber but couldn't quite make it. The first time I used this rig was in Long Island's Great South Bay, and in less than a half-hour a 6-pound Striper swallowed it—bobber and all!

WEAKFISH

Have you ever heard of an angler speak of catching "salt-water Trout"? If so, he wasn't talking through his hat; he was referring to the Weakfish, called Trout by many fishermen along the Atlantic Coast. "Weaks" are only fair fighters but they compensate for this lack of talent by being so numerous that when you find a school you can catch more than you can carry. For this reason, and because of his fair size—which averages 2 to 5 pounds, occasionally 10—the Weakfish ranks close to the top among salt-water game fish. Of course he has taste appeal, too. Commercial fishermen net over 25 million pounds of Weaks annually. And he has a cooperative habit of invading inshore waters where anglers on docks, bridges and in small boats have little trouble reaching him.

He has been named Weakfish because his mouth is paper-thin and easily torn. Remember this when you hook him—play him easy; don't try to muscle him in or you'll lose him. Actually there are many members of the world's Weakfish family, but the two most sought by anglers are residents of the Atlantic Coast. The northernmost of this pair roams between Massachusetts and Florida and is called just Weakfish. The other is the Spotted Weakfish which remains south of Delaware because he can't stand cold water. He literally can't stand it; when a cold snap catches him, he becomes numb and you can pick up the entire school with your hands! The Weakfish has a lethal look in spite of the fact that his mouth tears easily; his lower jaw protrudes pugnaciously and his upper jaw carries two large fangs. His color is silver-blue on back and silver-pink on the sides, with a thick scattering of black dots. The Spotted Weakfish looks the same except his spots are heavier and more conspicuous. The sure way to tell them apart is by their fins; the plain Weakfish has scales on his dorsal and anal fins while his spotted brother doesn't. The world record plain Weakfish was caught off New Jersey and weighed 17½ pounds; the world record Spotted Weak was a Florida fish weighing 15 pounds, 3 ounces.

The warm weather between May and October is the time to go Weak-fishing. Then he's spawning. And he's quite noisy about it; he's one of the few fish that can make actual grunting sounds. Specifically, only the male "speaks." Inlets and channels are his favorite inshore spawning spots. He feeds anywhere; when food is scarce in the bays he frequents the "rip" where two tides meet, or even the surf—places where the violence of the water puts his small prey more at his mercy. And he feeds on almost anything but prefers crabmeat, shrimp and squid. When still-fishing with bait, any tackle will do, but be sure each hook (about No. 2 for most Weaks) is tied to a twisted nylon snell heavy enough to be safe from his sharp teeth. Rig a sinker on the end of your line and tie the hooks above it, then bait up, cast out and let the bait roll on the bottom with the tide. If it doesn't roll enough, keep it moving by jerking it. Examine your hooks frequently because the crabs steal your bait.

The angler who still-fishes for Weaks, however, is missing a grand opportunity. No salt-water fish will take artificial lures, from flies to small plugs, more eagerly. Use fly tackle, spinning tackle or light bait-casting tackle, with leaders of not less than 10-pound-test because a Weakfish strikes hard. Besides, from the ocean's generous horde, you might collect some other species. Large streamer flies in red, white and yellow work well. For spinning, use weighted feather jigs in similar colors, and also small polished spinners and wobblers. Do the same for your light bait-casting outfit. On each lure add a piece of the real thing —shrimp or crabmeat—but not so much that it spoils the lure's action. When the tide is flowing away from you, especially if you're fishing from a dock, you can take advantage of the current. On your way to your fishing spot, get a bucket of grass shrimp, chopped clams or some prepared "chum." Before fishing, make a "chum slick" to draw the fish. Do this simply by dropping the chum into the water, a little at a time as the current carries it away, until finally there's a slick (or trail of "chum") extending out into the channel or bay. When the fish find it, they'll stay in it, eating the particles of bait which drift toward them. Now, cast your fly or small spinning lure into this slick. They'll hit it!

Bait-casting for Weaks isn't widely practiced because it's hard to get lures that are both small enough and heavy enough for this tackle. But there's a solution, and veteran Weakfishermen claim it'll take fish when all other baits and lures miss. Take the hooks off a colorful fresh-water Bass plug, one of the underwater darting kind, and tie it to your line. Then to its rear screw-eye, now hookless, tie 3 feet of 10-pound-test leader and to the end of this leader tie one of the small feathered spinning jigs with a dab of bait on its hook. And toss this setup into your

chum slick! The heavy plug will give you enough weight for a long cast, and the feathered jig is small enough for a Weakfish to grab. Besides, it's a strange thing about Weaks—nothing seems to make them madder than the sight of a small fish chasing a big one!

Part 3—

Fishing Methods

FLY-CASTING

Think you have to be a magician to cast a fly? It may look that way, especially when you're watching an expert do it. But fly-casting really is easy, although not as easy as spin-casting or bait-casting. And when you've mastered it, it will pay off in greater sport when your fish are the smaller species because fly tackle can be made lighter than any other kind and it gives your fish more of a fighting chance. You wouldn't be able to do much running if you were tethered to a flagpole and had a ball and chain tied to your ankle; similarly, a hooked fish can't do much fighting when the rod is too stiff and he has to drag with him a bunch of heavy sinkers or a heavy lure! Some fly rods are so limber that a breath of air will bend them. Of course there are heavy-duty fly rods, too, but even these are "light" tackle compared to the 10- to 20-pound, and larger, fish they must fight.

The Rod

Split-bamboo fly rods are still preferred by expert casters in spite of the growing popularity of "glass," which is really fiberglass. Glass is too "soft" (not stiff enough) for casting long distances. The extra "backbone" (stiffness) of split-bamboo is what gives the rod its casting power. But split-bamboo rods, which are handmade of strips glued together, are much more expensive than machine-made glass ones! Until you become an expert, it may be wiser for you to pay the much lower price for the glass rod which is only slightly inferior to bamboo. Rod length is seldom important. Anglers used to think 9-footers were necessary for good casting; now even $7\frac{1}{2}$ feet is not too short. The shorter rods are stiffer, too, and therefore more powerful. So are the heavier ones, but they'll tire your casting arm. Fly rods usually come in two or three sections which fit together by means of metal connections called "ferrules." Never twist the rod sections when putting them together or taking them apart since it might loosen these ferrules; always use a straight pull or push. The silk windings on a rod are pretty but don't make it any better. The fly rod's steel guides are called "snake" guides because of their twisted shape.

The Reel

The fly reel is the least important part of your casting outfit. All it

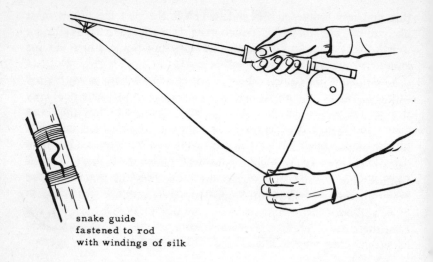

snake guide
fastened to rod
with windings of silk

does is hold the line; only when you fight very big fish do you have to turn it while "playing" them. Avoid large reels because they're heavy, unless you need the extra size to hold a lot of line, such as a "backing" line. This is 50 or 100 yards of cheap, strong nylon line tied to the end of your fly line so you'll have enough for a big fish that might run out a long distance. Your fly reel should have a simple "click" device so it won't unwind by itself.

The Line

Your fly line is the most important item of your tackle. If you have the right one, casting is easy, even if you're just a beginner. The standard fly line is about 30 yards long, made of enameled silk or treated nylon with a very smooth finish so it will slide through the rod's guides easily. And it must be heavy, because in fly-casting you don't really cast the fly—you cast the line. The fly just follows along! This weight, or thickness, is specified by letters of the alphabet from "A," the thickest and heaviest, to "G," the thinnest and lightest. It can be a "level" line, having the same thickness over its entire length, or a "double taper" which is thicker in the middle, tapering to thinner line at each end. Such a double taper is an "HEH," which is "H" thickness at the ends and "E" in the middle. The reason for its design is that it's thin and less visible on the end, which is the part the fish is most likely to see, but still heavy enough in its main section to have sufficient weight for casting. And when one end wears out, you can turn the line around on the reel and use the other end!

The third type of line is the real secret behind good casts; it's the "torpedo taper." It consists of three thicknesses in the same line: very thin on the fishing end (for about 3 feet), tapering to very thick and heavy line for the next 38 feet, then tapering to a medium-thick line for the remainder of 49 feet which is tied to your reel. Such a line is an "HCG." The torpedo taper's advantage? The thick, heavy part is right up front where it gives you a perfect weight concentration for casting. Lines made by different manufacturers may differ slightly in

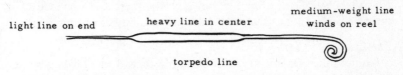

light line on end   heavy line in center   medium-weight line winds on reel

torpedo line

the lengths of the three sections, but the differences are insignificant. You must choose a torpedo taper to fit your rod, however. The stiffer the rod, the heavier the line needed. To solve this problem, ask your tackle dealer for help. By testing your rod, he'll know which line you should have.

Your fly line must be kept soft, pliable and free from cracks so that it will slide unhindered through the rod's guides. Lubricate it often with line dressing which you can buy at the tackle store. This dressing also helps the line to float, which is necessary when fishing dry flies. To be sure they'll float, some lines now are made with hollow cores. There's still another type designed for extra-long casting for fish that don't care if your line floats or not—a lead-core line. The purpose of the lead core, of course, is to add weight for the cast. Only exceptionally powerful, stiff rods will handle this type of line.

The Leader

The purpose of a fly leader is to serve as a connection, as invisible as possible, between your fly and your line. The longer and thinner the leader, the more invisible it will be. But there are limits to its length; 12-foot and 9-foot leaders are difficult to cast because they lessen the weight up front. And thin leaders aren't very strong. In general, use as long a leader as you can cast satisfactorily. Leaders used to be made of gut; now nylon is preferred because it's stronger, more durable and can be tapered smoothly from a thick length where it joins the fly line to a spider-web thinness where it is tied to the fly. Gut leaders were tapered by knotting together pieces of different thicknesses. The fine end of the leader that's tied to the fly is called the "tippet," and its size determines its breaking strength. These sizes range from "OX" (2-pound-test) to "7X" ($\frac{1}{4}$-pound-test). The commonest size for dry-fly fishing is "4X" ($\frac{5}{8}$-pound-test); for wet-flies, "2X" (1-pound-test). Strong plastic leader material of incredible thinness recently became available to anglers. To make it even more invisible, it is dyed blue or ash color. Although fly lines must float, especially for dry-fly fishing, all leaders must sink. Since nylon is waterproof, leaders made of it must be rubbed with a special "sink" preparation before they're used.

The Lure

Artificial flies are intended to imitate insects and small fish. The dry fly resembles a live fly that has just hatched from the water or fallen on the surface; the wet fly is the drowned fly being swept downstream by the current. The small, less colorful dry and wet patterns look most real—and get the most strikes—such as the Light Cahill, Dark Cahill, Black Gnat, etc. The bright colors usually attract more fishermen than

dry fly   wet fly

fish, but there are exceptions; when fish become "ornery" they seem to take the unreal patterns just for spite. What natural flies could the Scarlet Ibis, the red Parmachene Belle or rainbow-like Silver Doctor imitate? Yet they've all taken their share of fish on occasion.

The streamer flies are intended to imitate small minnows on which the fish feed. They're more difficult to cast than dry or wet flies because they're bulkier, meeting greater air resistance which slows up your line during the cast and throws off your timing. Still another fly that fish love is the nymph. It imitates a fly that is still in its underwater larval stage before it hatches into a flying insect. Actually the hellgrammite is the nymph of a fly called the "Dobson." Trout depend largely on nymphs for food during the early spring days when other insects are scarce. Your best artificial patterns are the Caddis Case (Caddis fly nymph), the May-fly nymph and the Stone-fly nymph.

The Knot

The standard knot for tying a fly to a nylon tippet is shown in the drawing—after threading the hook's eye, twist the end around the leader several times, pass it through the loop formed just above the hook's eye, then pull it tight. To keep the knot from pulling loose, touch a lighted cigarette to the end of the tippet; this will form a small blob of plastic which can't pull through.

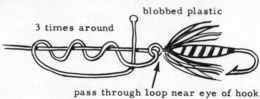

blobbed plastic

3 times around

pass through loop near eye of hook

How to Cast

To get the "feel" of your fly tackle, assemble your rod, reel and torpedo line without a leader. The reel should hang below the rod's handle, or "grip." Stand in an open space and pull out about 20 feet of line beyond your rod tip. Grasp your rod with one hand; with the other, hold the line that hangs from the reel so no more of it will pull out. Now flip the line that extends from your rod tip from side to side in a constant motion, letting the whippy rod do the flipping. Don't move the rod tip very far from the vertical position. Flip the line with a wrist action while you hold your elbow close to your side. Note how the line will curl out one side in a loop, and then, if you wait until just the right moment—just before the loop has straightened—a slight snap of your wrist will pull it in and roll it out the other side. This is your "timing." Practice until it's perfect, then try casting a longer line. Next, turn your cast so it's front and back instead of side to side, and "feel" the timing instead of watching the line. In either a forward cast (when the loop is rolling out in front) or a back cast (loop rolling out in back), if you snap the rod in the opposite direction too soon or too late, the line will simply wrap around your neck. Your timing must be in a

85

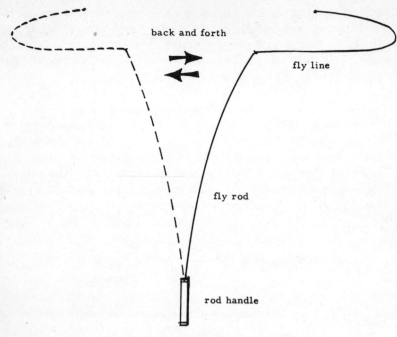

back and forth

fly line

fly rod

rod handle

Exercise to practice timing a cast

"1-2-3" count for both front cast and back cast—"1," the snap of the wrist that curls the line outward; "2," the hesitation until it uncurls just the right amount; and "3," the snap that brings it curling in the opposite direction.

Add a leader and a tuft of cotton to imitate a fly. The timing will remain the same. Only the length of line will alter that. Now, on one of your forward casts, let the line fall ahead of you. Just before it touches the ground, lift the rod tip a few inches so it tugs on the line slightly; the leader will curl ahead of the line and the cotton will fall first—just the way you'll want a fly to fall when you're fishing. To prepare for the next cast, pull in the slack line, raise your rod quickly and the line will lift over your head and curl behind you in a back cast. Notice that your back cast takes as much room in back of you as your forward cast does in front. Remember to cast high and vertically to keep the line over your head. Casting back and forth without letting the fly fall is

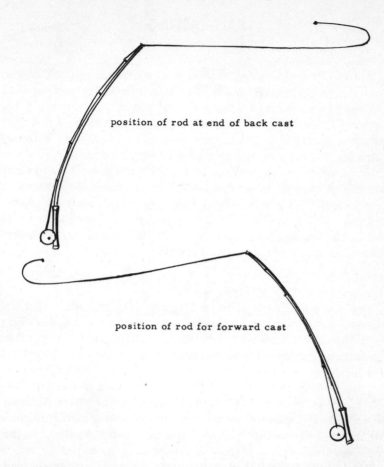

position of rod at end of back cast

position of rod for forward cast

called "false casting." It is used to dry a fly which has become water-logged, or to work out line for a cast. For extra distance, work out the line as far as you can, then pull off several yards more, looping it in your hand. Then, at the end of your forward cast, let these loops go and the extra line will "shoot" out through the guides. Retrieve this extra line before picking up your regular length for the next cast. Retrieving a line is done with one hand; twist your hand back and forth, grasping a few inches of line and pulling it in with each twist. This is the way to work a wet fly. It's also how you retrieve slack line without letting go of it while you're playing a fish.

BAIT-CASTING

Bait-casting is the fishing method most sportsmen use. It's easy to learn and its tackle is inexpensive. And it isn't limited to catching small fish, as fly-casting and spinning are unless you're an expert. A big cannibal Trout will hit your bait-casting spoon or plug. So will a hefty citizen of the sea such as a Striped Bass, and between these extremes there are hundreds of species willing to do the same. Accuracy is a great advantage of this tackle. Soon you'll be able to sight your casting rod the way you do a rifle and hit the target every time. Distance is another advantage; you can cast 150 feet or more with almost no effort— if you let your springy rod do the casting for you instead of trying to make your arm do all the work. Also, with bait-casting you don't need a lot of room behind you as in fly-casting.

The Rod

Your rod can be made of either fiberglass or split-bamboo. Both are suitable, but glass is better. Bamboo is more expensive and glass isn't as likely to snap when a big fish bends it in half. A long rod (6 to 7 feet) has more spring than a shorter one and with a light reel it will cast lures weighing as little as $\frac{1}{2}$ ounce, such as the ones you use for large panfish. For the $\frac{5}{8}$-ounce to 1-ounce plugs and spoons used to lure big Pike, Black Bass, and so forth, you'll need a stiffer rod of 5 or $5\frac{1}{2}$ feet. Although on a fly rod and spinning rod the reel hangs downward from the rod's handle, on a bait-casting rod the reel must be on top where you can reach its spool with your thumb. Therefore, this rod must have a reliable locking gadget to clamp the reel and keep it from slipping. It's usually a threaded band which screws out and over one end of the reel's base after the other end of the base has been slipped under a flange in the reel-seat. Make sure a bait-casting rod has some locking arrangement similar to this before you buy it.

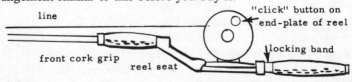

Side view of reel mounted on rod

Guides are important on a bait-casting rod. On a cast, the line shoots through them at terrific speed, so they must be absolutely smooth or else their friction will gradually wear and fray the line. Then, some day that prize fish you fight almost to the net will snap off and give you his fish-laugh. Polished steel guides, which are all right for light spinning lines and slow-moving fly lines, are only second-best for bait-casting lines. Your guides should be made of uncracked agate, the genuine hard mineral, not ordinary glass. Or else they should be made of one of the new crackproof plastics. This is especially important for the tip guide over which the shooting line passes at an angle, generating the most friction and wear. To assemble your rod, hold its sections so their guides line up perfectly with each other, then push—don't twist—the rod sections together. Guides out of alignment will cause more line wear.

The Reel

The bait-casting reel is a tricky little gadget. Once you've learned to control it, the rest of bait-casting is a cinch because it's the main part of the whole operation. A fly-casting reel simply holds the line; a spinning reel just holds the line and then winds it in after it's been cast; but a bait-casting reel does three things—stores line, lets it out, and pulls it in. It fastens to the top of your rod handle, its double-handle crank on the right (left on left-handed reels). Turn this crank and note how the spool of the reel revolves. It turns faster, usually about four turns for each turn of the crank. It's a "multiplying" reel—it multiplies the turns of the crank handle so you can reel in a lure quickly at a small fish's natural swimming speed. Reels come in different sizes which determine the length of line they'll hold on their spools. This information can be obtained from the folders which accompany them.

As you turn the crank, you'll also notice in the front of the reel a slotted device that moves from side to side. This is the "level wind" which distributes the line evenly on the spool as you wind it in. If it weren't for that, the line would build up in a mound on one spot on the spool, reducing the spool's capacity and slipping into an impossible snarl. On the side of the reel opposite the crank handle is a small sliding button—the "click" adjustment. Push it one way and the spool and handle can be turned freely; push it the other way and you'll hear a distinct "click" as they turn. This "click" is like a car's parking brake;

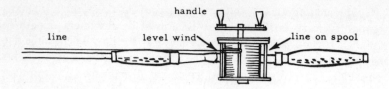

Top view of reel mounted on rod

it keeps the spool from unwinding when not in use. Push the "click" to "off" before casting. Large reels, such as those used for surf-casting, necessarily have large, heavy handles and so they also have a built-in arrangement to keep these big handles from windmilling during a cast. Such a reel is called a "free spool." Before the cast, the handle is turned slightly forward. This disengages it from the spool. Therefore, when the cast is made, only the spool revolves, not the handle. For the retrieve, the first backward turn of the handle re-engages it and the line is reeled in as usual. Large reels also have an adjustable "drag," or brake, to protect the line. This drag allows the spool to slip and release the line before it breaks when a fish pulls too hard, even when the angler may still be reeling in with all his strength.

The Line

Bait-casting line used to be made of silk until nylon, with its greater strength for its size, greater hardness and greater resistance to mildew, showed itself to be far superior. It comes in various strengths and lengths, dyed all different colors for camouflage. Green or black seems to be least visible to fish. For most fresh-water Bass casting, an 8-pound-test line is strong enough. Use as light a line as you can because the heavier it is, the more difficult it is to cast and the shorter your casts will be. However, for fish larger than Bass you'll have to settle for stronger, heavier line. In order to make casting as easy as possible, the line should fill the spool of your reel almost to its edges. But 100 yards of 8-pound-test only cover the bottom of a standard spool! The answer is to use a "backing"—more line to fill the spool partially before you wind your casting line on it. This can be an old or cheap line since it probably will never see action. Before it could, some Bass would have to run away with all 100 yards of your good line, which isn't likely. But a Muskie might! As a safety measure, tie the backing tightly to the spool of your reel and after winding it on, make sure to tie it securely to your casting line.

The Lure

There are thousands of lures for bait-casting—plugs that splash and gurgle, that perform on the surface and at all depths, and that imitate everything from small fish to swimming ducklings. Some recent ones look as though they might have come from Mars. There are also spoons of all descriptions that wobble fast and wobble slow, with and without hindquarters of colored feathers. They all catch fish and all are easy to cast. Spoons, especially, cast like bullets. Use them when you have to cast into a high wind. Use a "snap" (it looks like a small safety pin) at the end of your line to make changing lures easy—and change them often. With every snap there's a "swivel" to keep your line from being twisted by a revolving lure.

swivel

How to Cast

For your first bait-casting attempt, cast a $\frac{5}{8}$-ounce rubber practice plug you can buy at your tackle shop. Assemble your rod and reel, being sure to pass the line through the level-wind slot of the reel before threading it through the rod guides. Tie the plug to the line and let it hang about 8 inches from the rod tip. Now, turn the rod so the reel is upright and grasp the rod handle with one hand, holding it so your thumb can rest on the spool of the reel. Holding the spool tight with your thumb, push the "click" button to "off" with your other hand. Next, release your thumb. The spool unwinds as the plug falls and pulls out line. But what happens when the plug hits the ground? The spool got started; there's nothing to stop it; it keeps right on turning. The line on it loosens and snarls. That, friend, is the curse of bait-casters—the "backlash"—but you have only a little one. Wait until you fumble a cast and get a king-size one! Straighten out your line, wind it in and do it again, but this time press your thumb on the spool as soon as the plug touches the ground to keep the spool from over-running. No snarl! That's what your thumb must do during your cast: it must act as a brake to keep the spool from unwinding faster than the plug is pulling out line, and it must stop the spool completely before the plug touches the water.

Now let's try a short cast. With your thumb on the spool and the plug hanging about 8 inches from the rod tip, raise your rod and swish the plug in a fore-and-aft direction directly over your head, moving the rod tip back and forth only a yard or so each time. Notice how the spring of the rod keeps the lure moving! Now, just as the rod tip snaps the plug forward and just before the plug reaches its forward position, release your thumb so it exerts only a very slight pressure on the spool. The plug will sail out farther than you think! And if you've remembered to use your thumb to stop the spool before the plug drops, you won't get a backlash. Repeat this exercise, lengthening the casts by swishing a little harder until you've learned at which stage in the cast to release your thumb and when to start increasing the pressure on the spool again. For your next step, eliminate the swishing entirely. Point your rod tip ahead of you, sighting it at your target. Imagine there's an apple stuck on the tip and you're going to throw it. Bring the rod up and back sharply to your old swishing position, let the rod tip bend backward with the momentum of the plug, then bring the rod forward to about a 45-degree angle and release your thumb as the plug begins to pull forward—you know when from your swishing exercise. As the plug flies out, apply light thumb pressure to brake the reel slightly. When the plug is directly over the target, stop the spool so the plug will fall directly on it. Sounds easy—and it is! The whole secret is to educate

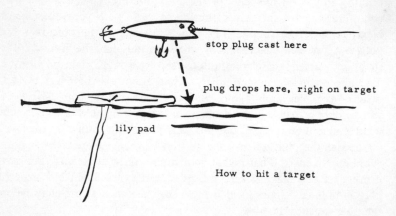

stop plug cast here

plug drops here, right on target

lily pad

How to hit a target

that thumb. Once you've done this, there are a couple of additional tricks. When you cast, turn your rod on its side so the reel is vertical with its crank handle on top. This puts the weight of the spool on the end bearing so it will turn more easily, and you'll get more distance. Also, keep pointing your rod tip at the lure as it flies through the air, to lessen the line friction at the tip guide. You might try some side casts, too, which come in handy when there are trees overhead. But overhead casting is most accurate—and safer—especially when you're casting with a companion in a boat.

When you get a backlash, don't yank the line from the spool in desperation. Pull gently while rolling the snarled line from side to side with your thumb and you'll gradually work it loose. To reel in a lure, or when playing a fish, you switch hands. Take the rod in your other hand and turn the reel crank with your first hand. Now your other thumb must control the spool—acting as an adjustable drag when a fish wallops your lure and starts to run with it.

SPINNING

Spinning is a fishing method that's rather new in this country. Brought here from England shortly after World War II, this method originated in France, where it has been called "light casting" because of the lightweight lures used. At first spinning caused some American anglers, especially the fly-fishermen, to panic, because it was such a deadly Trout-catcher, and they tried to have it declared illegal. Even now its use is prohibited in some waters. It's deadly not only because fish like its lures, but because spinning tackle is so easy to cast with that every angler becomes an expert. It's even simpler to use than bait-casting tackle, and in most cases can be used instead of it. Spinning tackle can also be used in places where fly-casting tackle can't, because a spinning rod doesn't require a lot of room for a cast. There is no back cast in spinning. It has one disadvantage, however. The size of spinning line is limited, and this limits its strength. Therefore spinning tackle isn't recommended for general fishing where there are lily pads, weeds and snags because the fish will break off easily. You'll lose too many.

The Rod

Spinning requires a special rod between 6 and 8 feet long with a very stiff tip. Before buying a spinning rod, test it by switching it back and forth with a fast snapping motion. After each switch, the tip should snap straight again instantly with no lag. A rod made of split-bamboo will have a stiffer tip than one made of glass, but will be more expensive. Glass spinning rods perform almost as well and are cheaper. The advantage of a short rod (6 feet) is that it's easier to cast with when you're surrounded by bushes and overhead tree limbs. It doesn't need as much space for your casting swing. You can recognize a spinning rod by its cork "grip" or handle on which the reel fastens by means of two sliding metal bands. You can recognize it also by its first line-guide above the grip; it's huge, almost an inch in diameter. The line "spins" through it during the cast. The remaining guides, about 4, are smaller and vary in size. The tip guide is the smallest.

The Reel

The spinning reel is an amazing little machine, although it looks clumsy. Some anglers call it a "coffee mill" or "grinder," and it really

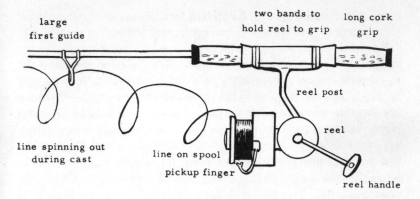

large
first guide

two bands to
hold reel to grip

long cork
grip

reel post

reel

line spinning out
during cast

line on spool

pickup finger

reel handle

Spinning reel assembly

does look like one with its big handle and its long post which makes it project almost 6 inches from the rod's grip. Its spool, which holds the line, is "fixed"—it doesn't turn during the cast. One end of this spool faces the front of the rod. During the cast, the line slips out over the edge, or "lip," of this front end of the spool with a "spinning" motion. This is the reel's secret! The line leaves it freely, with almost no resistance. It doesn't have to turn the spool and a handle as it goes. If it weren't for air resistance, your spinning reel would let you cast a lure a mile—almost! Also, you don't have to stop the spool and handle with your thumb at the end of a cast. When the lure hits the water and stops, the line automatically stops also. There's no overrunning of spool and handle to cause a backlash. You can't backlash a spinning reel. Your thumb is out of a job!

When you turn the reel's handle to retrieve the line, a wire loop called a "bail" (or a curved metal finger called a "pickup") snaps over the line, catches it and turns around the spool, winding it back on like magic. Since spinning reels are multipliers like bait-casting reels, each turn of the handle winds 4 or 5 turns of line on the spool. The reel also has an adjustable "drag," or brake. This protects the line from breaking when a fish pulls too hard. With the bail or pickup in place, the line can't uncoil from the spool when the fish pulls—but the brake allows the spool to slip and turn on its axis like a bait-casting reel's spool, and the line is pulled out in spite of the pickup. A better name for this brake would be "clutch" because it actually regulates the amount of pull required before the spool will slip and turn. Before fishing, you must set this drag so that it's less than the breaking strength of your line.

Before each cast, the bail or pickup is snapped out of the way so the line will be able to spin from the spool. Since nothing moves on the reel during the cast, there is no need for you to touch it with your fingers. The long base post holds it away from the rod grip where the line can spin off without interference. The reel is attached so it hangs below the cork grip. Where you place it on this long grip depends upon where you "feel" it balances best when you hold the rod. Most anglers prefer it just forward of the center position.

The Line

Spinning line is made of monofilament (single-strand nylon), or of braided nylon strands, dyed blue, green or gray to make them invisible to a fish. This line must be light and fine, almost as thin as thread, so it will have no weight to slow up its spinning from the reel or to slow up the lure as it flies through the air during the cast. One of 3- or 5-pound-test is strong enough for most panfishing in open water. It can even hold a 10-pounder if you "baby" him and let your rod absorb his sudden twists and leaps. As the water gets weedier and the fish get large, however, it's best to use a heavier line, perhaps one of 10-pound-test, although it will shorten your casts slightly. Such a line should be powerful enough to hold a Musky or Striped Bass—if you have enough of it. The spool of a standard size spinning reel holds about 200 yards of medium-test line. This should fill the spool *almost* to its "lip," or edge. If the line on the spool is more than $\frac{1}{16}$-inch below this lip it will catch on the lip and won't spin off freely. If it's piled up higher than the lip it will slide off in coils and will snarl. When you have too much line, cut off the surplus. When you don't have enough, add some "backing" line as described in the chapter on bait-casting. For very large fish, including the salt-water species, you can get a king-size spinning reel that will hold all the line necessary for their long runs. Such reels work well for surf-casting, too.

Be careful of kinking, or accidentally knotting, a monofilament line since kinks and knots will reduce its strength to at least half. There aren't many knots you can use for tying a lure to monofilament without weakening it—the one described for attaching leaders in the chapter on fly-casting is the best and safest. Although your spinning line won't backlash, it can cause you trouble in another way—it can get twisted by a lure that revolves steadily in the water, or you can accidentally give it a twist as you first wind it on your reel when it's new. Then it will form kinky loops instead of remaining straight and pliable. And these loops, spinning from the spool during a cast, will snarl and might catch in the guides, snapping the line. To avoid a twist when fishing, always use a swivel or two between your line and lure. If there is a twist on your line, remove the lure and let out all the line behind a moving boat; its motion through the water will untwist it. To avoid a twist when putting a new line on your reel, wind the line by hand and after every 10 windings turn over the original spool the line is wound on so it comes off first from one side, then from the other.

The Lure

More lures are made for spinning than for any other kind of casting. They even outnumber the artificial-fly patterns. Fly-casters poke fun at them and call them "jewelry." Truthfully, some of them do look like fancy lockets or earrings. They certainly don't imitate anything a fish has ever seen in nature. Only half of them resemble minnows even slightly. But, mysteriously, they all catch fish! Maybe the fly-casters are just angry because a Trout can be so smart about flies, but so dumb about spinning lures.

With spinning tackle you can cast bait such as minnows, worms, frogs and so forth. Most of these are heavy enough for use without any added weight such as a sinker. A bobber can be used if desired. But the artificial lures catch almost as many fish and are more fun to use. Try spoons, plugs, wobblers, spinners or weighted flies—anything from $\frac{1}{8}$- to $\frac{3}{4}$-ounce, even most bait-casting lures. They all cast easily. You can even cast a dry fly or wet fly with spinning tackle, a fact that makes Trout fishermen very unhappy. Tie the heavy torpedo section of a torpedo-tapered fly line to the end of your spinning line, and add to the fly line the regular fly leader and fly. Then, with your forefinger holding the spinning line as usual, false cast (see the section on fly-casting) the fly-line rig overhead with your spinning rod, timing it just as though it were a fly rod and you were getting ready to cast it that way. But, when you have the fly line looping back and forth with good timing, release your forefinger on a forward swing and out she'll fly. You'll get more distance with that fly than you ever did with conventional fly tackle. All the spinning rod needs is the slight extra weight to cast, and the fly line added to the fly supplies that.

How to Cast

Ready to discover why spinning is so easy? Assemble your rod sections by lining up the guides, then by pushing—not twisting—the ferrules together. Fasten the reel to the grip by means of the two sliding bands, thread the line through the guides and tie to its end a very light sinker ($\frac{1}{4}$ ounce) or a spinning lure from which you've removed the hooks. Now grasp the rod grip just above the reel, your thumb along the top of the grip, your forefinger in front of the base of the reel and your remaining three fingers in back of it. With your free hand, crank the reel handle until the bail or pickup is at a bottom position, then reach downward with the forefinger of the hand that's holding the rod and hook that finger around the line. Lift the line with it and hold the line against the rod grip so the lure can't pull it out. Then, with your free hand, snap the bail or pickup out of the way. You're ready to cast—but first let's see how the reel works.

Point the rod ahead of you and release the line you're holding with your forefinger. The lure will fall and the line will spin out. But when the lure hits the ground and stops, the line will stop also. There'll be no backlash. Now for the retrieve. Crank the reel handle with your free hand. The bail or pickup will automatically snap back into position, hook the line and wind it back on the spool. Reel in the lure until it's about 8 inches from the rod tip and prepare for a real cast. Hold the line with your forefinger as before, snap the bail or pickup out of the way and swish the lure back and forth over your head. Note how the springiness of the rod tugs on the lure. Select some target about 100 feet distant and on one of the forward motions of your rod, when it is pointed only slightly above this target, release your forefinger. (A large basket is a good target to practice on—or a hula hoop.) If you've released the line too soon, it will climb like a little Atlas missile and disappear over a treetop. This is what usually happens to an angler used to bait-casting tackle when he tries spinning for the first time, because the timing is different. A bait-casting lure must be released sooner in the casting swing because it's slower getting started due to the drag of the reel spool and handle which it has to start turning. If you've released the line too late, however, as most beginners do on their first try, the lure will hit the ground at your feet. But after a few tries, you'll quickly learn the right timing. Then when you point your rod tip at a target (which might be the swirl of a big Bass), snap the lure over your head

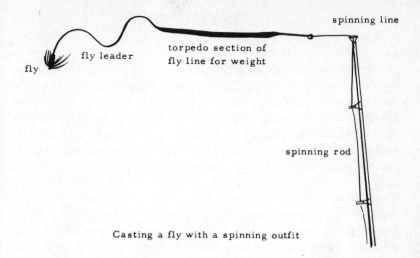

spinning line

fly leader

fly

torpedo section of
fly line for weight

spinning rod

Casting a fly with a spinning outfit

and let the rod tip snap it forward again, it'll shoot out for a bull's-eye every time. When you see that your lure is going to overshoot the spot you've aimed for—you've cast it too far—it's simple to stop it. Just grab the line with your free hand as it spins out. Or crank the handle once so the pickup will hook the line and stop it. After you've learned the straight overhead cast, you can try the variations—side casts, underhand casts, bow casts, and the rest. They're all just as simple.

SPIN-CASTING

Spin-casting is the newest of all the fishing tricks. It's not the same as spinning, although spinning is casting, too. Spin-casting is a technical term (to anglers) and it refers to a method that's really a combination of spinning and bait-casting. With it you use spinning line, either a spinning or bait-casting rod, and either spinning or bait-casting lures. It's made possible by a special little device called the spin-cast reel. And as you can guess, this reel is also a combination.

The Reel

In recent years, designers have been trying to perfect a reel that's better than all the others. The objection to the bait-casting reel is that the spool, which is full of line, and the reel handle turn during the cast. This means you must have an educated thumb to control it. It also means the rod must be stiffer to cast the heavy lures which are necessary to turn the spool and handle, and a stiff rod doesn't give a fish as much of a fightin' chance. You don't have as much fun catching him. The spinning reel solves these problems, but presents others. It's clumsy, projecting far out from the rod handle. In such a position it's more likely to strike something accidentally and become damaged, especially the bail or pickup. The angler's greatest criticism of it is that it projects so far from the rod that when you're playing a large fish with it and turning its handle, it's almost impossible to keep the rod from twisting

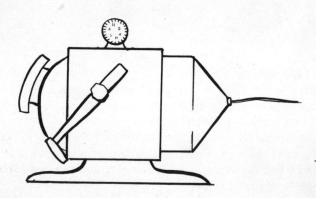

from side to side in your hand. Wouldn't it be nice to have a reel that was as rugged and compact as the bait-casting type, and as foolproof as the spinning type? The engineers thought so. Several years ago they perfected it—the spin-cast reel. Now you can choose from a dozen different brands.

The spin-cast reel mounts on a bait-casting rod exactly like a bait-casting reel. On a spinning rod it goes on just like a spinning reel except that you turn the rod upside down so the reel is on top instead of hanging down below the grip. Its handle is like that of a bait-casting reel. But the spool that holds the spinning line has one end facing the front like that of a spinning reel. And it is completely enclosed by a cover with only a small hole in its front center through which the line passes during the cast. Because of this cover, the spin-cast reel is sometimes referred to as a "closed-face" spinning reel. At the back of the reel is a button or lever within easy reach of your thumb. This controls the cast. The spin-cast reel also has a drag which works like that on the regular spinning reel.

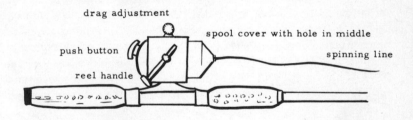

The Line

Since a spin-cast reel uses spinning line, there's a limit to the strength of the line you can use. You'll cast best with a light line of 10-pound-test or less. And avoid twisting it with revolving lures or when winding it on your spin-cast reel. Follow the instructions on twisted line in the chapter on Spinning. You can remove the cover of the spin-cast line easily for hand-spooling. Regardless of line weight, your stiff bait-casting rod is best for casting heavy bait-casting lures, and your spinning rod is best for spinning lures.

How to Spin-Cast

Casting with it is so easy your baby brother can do it. With your tackle assembled, reel in the lure until it's a few inches from the rod tip. Grasp the rod in back of the reel and rest your thumb on the reel's button or lever. Press it and hold it in. Now raise the rod tip quickly to a position over your head and slightly behind, and bring it forward in a cast. At the position where, with a spinning reel, you would pull back your forefinger to release the line, on the spin-cast reel you simply lift your thumb from the button. This frees the line and out shoots the lure. If you want to stop the lure during the cast, push on the button once more. This brakes it. To retrieve the lure, shift the rod to your other hand and wind the reel handle with your casting hand as you do with a bait-casting reel. The hidden line-pickup is automatic. When playing a fish you don't have to thumb the line spool; the adjustable drag takes care of that.

STILL-FISHING AND DOCK-FISHING

On a famous Trout stream in New England a city slicker with plenty of expensive fly tackle but not a single fish met a barefoot boy who had caught several huge Trout with a bent pin on a piece of string.

"What did you catch 'em on?" he asked.

"Mister, you can't improve on Nature!" answered the boy, holding up a can of fat worms.

It's more interesting, and more sport, to use the artificial fish-foolers, but seldom will any of them beat a piece of natural bait on your hook when you want to catch the most fish and the largest. Moreover, lures must be kept moving or they won't fool anything because it's their motion through the water that gives them a lifelike action. Even a dry fly must be given a realistic twitch or two so that old Mr. Trout will think it's still kicking. And to make lures move, you must troll them, or cast and retrieve them. Bait can be trolled, or cast and retrieved, too, but it isn't necessary. You don't have to help a worm squirm. Just drop him overboard and he'll do it by himself. So will a frog, crawfish, grass-hopper and all the others. This fishing without casting, while you let your bait do all the luring, is called "still-fishing," and it's the same whether you're dangling from a dock, or getting blisters from the hard seat of a rowboat, or lounging like Cleopatra on the soft cushions of a cabin cruiser.

Rods, Reels and Lines

Still-fishing requires no special tackle, but don't use an ordinary string because it might not be strong enough. And don't use a bent pin because it has no barb on its point to hold either the bait or fish. Your tackle can be a fly-casting, bait-casting, spinning or spin-casting outfit, or a simple hand line which is a length of fish line wound on a wooden or plastic holder. A rod, of course, will let your fish fight harder when he's hooked; with a hand line all you do is haul him in hand-over-hand. And a rod will enable you to cast your bait farther from the boat or dock. Use the same line that's on your casting outfit—unless it's an expensive fly line. Then it's wiser to save it for its specialized job of fly-casting, and substitute a cheap bait-casting line. Nylon lines are best for both fresh water and salt water. And level leaders are stronger than tapered ones.

Bobbers

A "bobber" is commonly used in fresh-water still-fishing. It's a float that attaches to your line and lets you know when a fish is tugging on your hook. In its simplest form, it's no more than a big cork with a slit in its side into which you wedge the line. Its distance from the hook determines how far the hook will sink. Bobbers sold in tackle stores are more elaborate but they work the same way. Some are pear-shaped and ride upright on the water. Others are long thin tubes that lie flat. Both types are brightly colored so you can see them clearly. The pear-shaped kind bobs up and down when a fish nibbles, and when it starts to move away, or disappears completely, you jerk the line to set the hook because then you know the fish has a firm hold on the bait. The tube kind stands straight up in the air when a fish nibbles, and ducks out of sight when he runs with it. The disadvantage of a bobber is that when

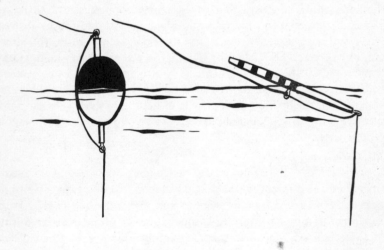

you're using it with a rod, you can't fish deep. Usually you can go no deeper than the length of your rod, because you can reel in only a certain length of line before the bobber strikes your top tip guide and stops. The only way you can get the hooked fish is to pull him in by hand. Some bobbers are made with hollow cores so they can slide down the line, but they're not easy to use. The salt-water still-fisherman, who almost always must fish deep, seldom bothers with a bobber.

Hooks

Hooks for still-fishing with a hand line or with bait-casting tackle, either in fresh water or salt water, should be the "snelled" kind. These are eyeless hooks, each with a 10- or 12-inch nylon leader, or "snell," fastened to its shank. At the other end of the snell is a loop to which you tie your line. The purpose of the snell is invisibility; since the fish can't see it, they're less suspicious of your baited hook. Snelled hooks can be used with fly-casting, spinning and spin-casting tackle, also, but they're not necessary. With fly-casting tackle you already have an invisible leader, and the monofilament lines of spinning and spin-casting reels also are invisible. In these cases, eyed hooks will serve just as well. For fish with sharp teeth, always still-fish with hooks that are snelled with heavy, twisted nylon. The fish will bite through them anyhow, but not as often—and without snells you're not likely to get any bites at all on a heavy line.

Hooks come in many sizes. For practical use, No. 6/0 is the largest. Next smaller is 5/0, then 4/0, etc., down to 1/0, after which the sizes start downward from No. 1 to No. 16 which is the smallest. The size you need depends upon two things: the size of the fish's mouth and the

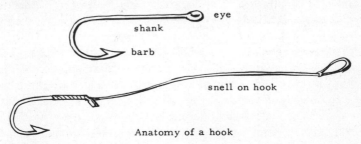

Anatomy of a hook

kind of bait you use. The hook with bait on it obviously must be small enough for the fish to grab. For example: the average Bluegill has a small mouth and takes about No. 6. But a Largemouth Black Bass can gobble a No. 2/0 with no trouble. Why not the small Bluegill hook for Bass ? Not recommended because a small hook is made of thin wire and is weaker than a large one. Besides, it has too small a curve and instead of penetrating a Bass's mouth, in most instances it will just catch under the skin and pull free easily. From the standpoint of bait, however, you frequently have to take your chances with a small hook because a large one will kill your bait too quickly. Bass like grasshoppers, but how long will a grasshopper stay alive on a big No. 2/0 Bass hook? Here it is better to settle for a Bluegill hook, or use one slightly larger and tie the grasshopper to it with thread.

An objection anglers frequently have to small hooks for bait is that fish usually swallow them completely and so are hooked inside the stomach instead of the mouth. Then, when a fish is smaller than legal size, it can't be returned to the water unharmed because it's impossible to unhook it without fatally injuring it. Mouth wounds are almost never fatal, but a fish must be cut open for the removal of a hook from its innards. Fish biologists have come up with a startling remedy, however. They recommend that when a small fish swallows your hook, cut the snell as far down its throat as possible, then return it to the water with the hook still in its stomach. They've found that in most such cases the hooks miraculously dissolve and the fish live.

Sinkers

Sinkers are made not only in different weights but also in different shapes because they have different purposes. Only one of these is to sink your baited hook down to where the fish are. Some sinkers are intended to supply a slight additional weight for casting. Others are used as small anchors to keep your hook from drifting with a strong current.

All sinkers are made of soft lead because this is the heaviest substance. The simplest shape is the split-shot, a small pellet (ranging from buckshot to BB size) which is split almost in half. For added weight in casting, you fasten it on your leader or monofilament line by squeezing the halves together. Another lightweight, easy-to-fasten type is the "wraparound." This is a thin strip of lead which you twist around your line or leader, instead of squeezing it on. These two are popular with users

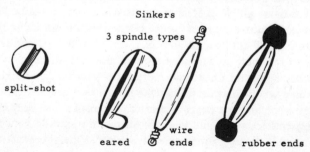

Sinkers

3 spindle types

split-shot

eared   wire ends   rubber ends

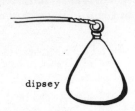

dipsey

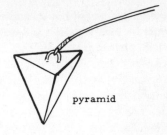

pyramid

of fly-casting and spinning tackle. To add weight to a bait-casting lure, or just to sink a baited hook, the commonest sinker design is the "spindle," an elongated sinker with a slot in its side and a flap of lead on each end. To fasten it, you put the line in the slot and under the flaps, then squeeze down the flaps to hold it. A variation of this type has no slot or flaps, but a spring-fastener at each end to hold the line. The latest variation has rubber ears on its ends; a simple and easy twist fastens the line behind them. Sinkers which fasten at the end of your line and are designed chiefly for anchoring your baited hook, come in assorted shapes. The "dipsey" is a popular non-snagging one. It's shaped like a pear with a swivel-ring at the stem end. Another is the "pyramid" which has the connecting ring in its flat base.

How to Still-Fish

In still-fishing, you must get your baited hook down to a level where the fish on the bottom can at least see it. If you're fishing where a bobber will allow you enough line to do this (at least a length equal to the length of your rod), use it because it will keep your hook away from your boat or dock when you cast it, and the fish that see the hook won't also see you. But make sure you are able to tell whether the bobber signals "bite" or just "nibble." When it dances up and down on the surface, fish are nibbling. Reel in the slack line and get ready. When the bobber goes under, or almost goes under, strike! Lift your rod tip high because there'll still be a lot of slack line you have to straighten before you can exert pull on the hook. If you miss the strike, don't reel in right away to put on a new bait. Let the hook rest a minute. Maybe the fish didn't get the bait, in which case he'll take it again. In still-fishing without a bobber, first lower a sinker to determine how deep the water is, then subtract 4 feet and measure off this distance on your fish line, tying a small slipknot in the line to mark it. When you cast out your baited hook, let out line to this mark, then let your hook gradually sink. When it's hanging straight down, it will be at just the right depth.

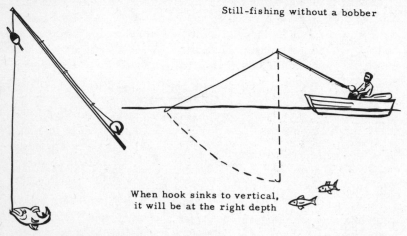

Still-fishing without a bobber

When hook sinks to vertical, it will be at the right depth

If you use too much line on your bobber, you can't reel in far enough to reach your fish

How to Dock-Fish

Dock-fishing is salt-water still-fishing, and it's part of a sport that ocean anglers refer to as "bottom-fishing." The principal difference between this and fresh-water still-fishing is that you don't have to worry as much about the bottom; it's usually sand with few places for your bait to hide. When bottom-fishing, always keep your line taut against the sinker that anchors it, and keep the line between two fingers. Your fingers will feel any vibration or tug that will indicate a bite. Reel in your hooks frequently to inspect them, because crabs and small fish will steal your bait continually.

TROLLING

Trolling is towing a lure behind a moving boat or canoe. Like still-fishing, it doesn't have much appeal to an active angler who isn't content to just "set," although it does give him a change of scenery as he trolls around a woodland lake or river. And if it's just exercise he's interested in, he can always row or paddle. But with the increasing popularity of outboard motors, almost everybody who trolls uses an outboard. And, surprisingly, experiments have proved that in water deeper than 10 feet a passing outboard motor doesn't alarm a fish the slightest bit. As a matter of fact, some species are attracted by its white wake. Trolling does have two definite advantages, no matter how many fly-casters, bait-casters and spinners frown on it—it enables an angler to cover a lot more water, and it enables him to find the haunts of the fish. After he's found them, he can use *any* fishing method.

Rods, Reels and Line

All tackle isn't suitable for trolling. For example, spinning tackle isn't very good, although some anglers use it with limited success. One of the reasons is that a fish seems to wallop a trolled lure harder than a cast one, then he immediately streaks away with it like a jet. And spinning line is too fragile to withstand such punishment. It's even too weak to hold the sinkers that usually are necessary in trolling. Even if it were stronger, the spinning reel isn't designed to protect it against a running fish. When a fish strikes your trolled lure, he can pull line from your reel in only two ways: when the pickup is released in casting position, in which case the line is completely free and he can take all of it in one swish; or by turning the spool against the drag, but the drag is only an emergency device. If set loose enough for a fish to take out line without snapping it, the drag would also be too loose for you to reel in the line, or to have any control over it. Spin-casting tackle has similar disadvantages. But bait-casting tackle is perfectly suited for trolling; fly-casting tackle is all right for small fish.

For large fresh-water species such as the Largemouth and Small-mouth Black Bass, the Pike family and large Trout, use a stiff 5 or $5\frac{1}{2}$ foot bait-casting rod—a shorter, even stiffer one for big salt-water fish. The line strength will vary according to the size of your fish, from 10-

pound-test for Black Bass to 30-pound-test or more for Muskies and Striped Bass. It's best to choose a trolling line that's stronger than your casting line because when the strike occurs it usually takes you by surprise and the strain on your tackle is greater. The main thing to remember about line, however, is to have enough of it. Your reel should be the bait-casting kind large enough to hold at least 100 yards of line of the required strength, even more for Stripers. In addition, use a wire leader between your lure and line when you're trolling for the toothy members of the Pike clan. You'll need sinkers, also, to take your lure down to the fish's depth. The "spindle" sinker attaches directly to your line above the lure, but if a heavier one is needed, use a "dipsey." Tie it to the line, about 3 feet above the lure, by means of a weaker line about a foot long. Then, if it snags, you can break it off without losing your lure.

Trolling with fly-casting tackle will provide you with plenty of action where there are panfish such as the Sunfishes, Bluegill and Perch, and the small salt-water species. Even small Rainbow and Brook Trout will hit when conditions are right. But use a heavy fly rod because it will take a beating. And make sure there's plenty of backing line on your fly reel. A 5-pound-test level leader will be strong enough, and if you need a sinker, use a split-shot or a wrap-around.

Lures

For large fresh-water or salt-water fish, use any of your deep-swimming bait-casting lures, adding sinkers ahead of each to get it down deep enough. In very deep water, luminous lures are good. Spoons are always fish-getters, especially when a strip of prepared pork rind is added to the hook. For large Lake Trout and the monster Rainbows of Lake Pend Oreille, a favorite trolling lure is a spinner that is sometimes called a "Christmas tree" because it looks like part of one—a series of large, flashing spinners and colored beads a yard long with a feathered treble hook or a baited single hook trailing them. A dead minnow or shiner, tied on a hook with some thread and fastened behind a spinner, is one of the best fish-getters. For panfish trolling with a fly rod, use a midget plug or spoon or a small spinner with a brightly colored fly behind it. Worms, small minnows or insect bait must be attached to small spinners, also, in order to attract panfish to them. Then they're killers.

How to Troll

Since trolling is a kind of exploring, unless you already know some good spots to troll over, try everywhere possible on a lake, river, or salt-water bay. Sunken weeds are promising, as are rocky bars that extend into the water from a point of land. Channels are also good spots. When you've gotten a strike while your lure was passing over a certain spot, make a large circle so you'll pass over it again. If you get fish from it, make a note of it. Chances are it's one of their haunts.

Depth is important in trolling and easy to regulate, but the selection of the right depth is often simply a guess. How do you know how deep to make your lure swim to be close to the bottom, when you don't know how deep the bottom is? Of course, in places where the depth is known, the problem is solved. You can regulate the depth of your lure by three means: by the speed of your boat (the faster you go, the closer to the surface your lure will troll), by the length of line you let out (the more line, the deeper the lure), and by the weight of the added sinkers. While trolling, you can vary two of these means to vary your lure's depth— when you come to a shallow bar or weed bed, speed up your motor and reel in some line to make the lure ride higher; when you're past the shallows, slow down and let her out again. Be careful of sharp turns; while a boat is turning, the lure turns in a much smaller circle, its forward motion slows and it sinks. In general, you should troll at least 100 feet of line.

deep hole -- slow up boat
and/or let out more line
so lure swims deeper

rocky bar -- speed up boat and/or reel in some
line to make lure come closer to surface

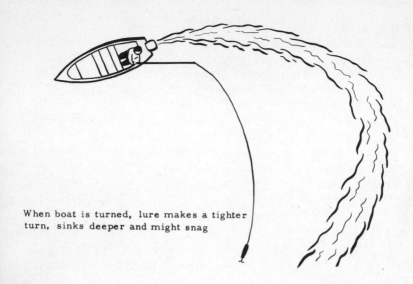

When boat is turned, lure makes a tighter turn, sinks deeper and might snag

Always troll with the click button of your bait-casting reel (or fly reel) in the "on" position so the line will be free for the fish to take when he strikes but won't be completely without a drag. If at all possible, keep your rod in your hand while trolling; don't lay it down to rest against the boat's gunwale because a sudden strike might snap its tip, or even yank it entirely out of the boat. Many a good rod has been lost to a Muskie or big Striper. There is no need to jerk your rod to set the hook when a fish hits your trolled lure; he hooks himself on the strike. An exception might be the iron-jawed Muskie; in his case always set the hook a few times—just to be sure!

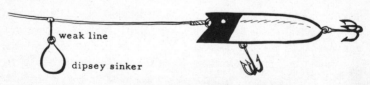

weak line

dipsey sinker

Weighting a lure for trolling deep

ICE-FISHING

When winter comes to the Northern states and the lakes and rivers freeze solid, you can try the most rugged fishing sport of all—ice-fishing. Of course you must be somewhat rugged yourself because standing in freezing temperatures and snow squalls for hours at a time isn't anyone's idea of comfort. But you can catch yourself a mess of fish. A surprising number of species bite in midwinter as well as mid-summer. They may not have as much pep because of the cold, but neither will you. There are Perch in the deep holes of the lake, and Pickerel or Pike in the shallows where the water is only a couple of feet deep. There are also Walleyes, Lake Trout and Bluegills, and even Eels where you're permitted to fish at night. You'll catch few Black Bass, however, because they seem to hibernate. Winter fishing for them is illegal in most states, anyhow. All ice-fishing generally is illegal in waters containing Trout other than Lakers. (CAUTION: A few anglers drown every year by falling through ice that's too thin. It must be at least 3 inches thick to be safe. Be especially careful near the shores of spring-fed lakes, near outlets and inlets, and wherever there's a moving current of water. Also, ice may be dangerously thin when it first freezes in fall, or when it's about to break up in spring.)

Tackle

You need an ice-ax or ice-chisel to chop your fishing hole, and an ice-skimmer to keep it free of slush and to break and remove any ice crust that might try to freeze over it. Any ax will serve the purpose, and a long-handled food strainer which you can buy in any hardware store makes a good skimmer. Rods and reels aren't necessary for ice-fishing—there's no room to use them. Instead you have a device called a "tilt" or "trap" or simply "tip-up," which stands in the ice alongside your fishing hole and holds your line. The simplest kind is a wooden frame with a small spool for the line, and a red flag tied to a spring. The spring is bent down and cocked under a latch, and the line that hangs through the fishing hole is looped over a trigger connected to the latch. When a fish tugs on the hook, the line pulls the trigger and the spring lifts the red flag to warn you. Then you take over the fishing by hand. You also have to pull in your fish by hand. Ice-anglers for Lake Trout have a unique way of landing their monster fish—they turn

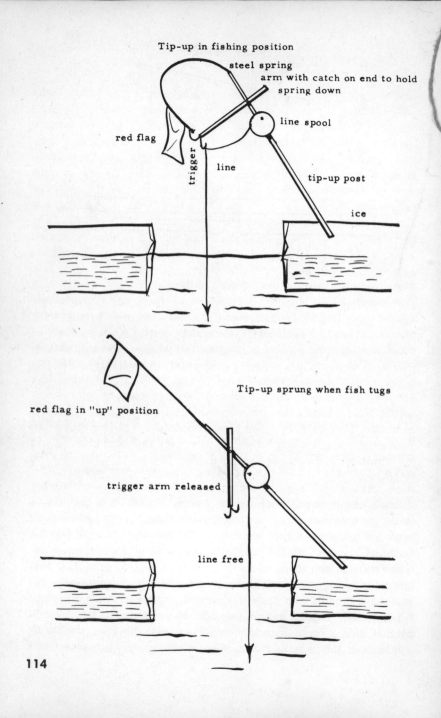

Tip-up in fishing position

steel spring

arm with catch on end to hold spring down

line spool

red flag

trigger

line

tip-up post

ice

Tip-up sprung when fish tugs

red flag in "up" position

trigger arm released

line free

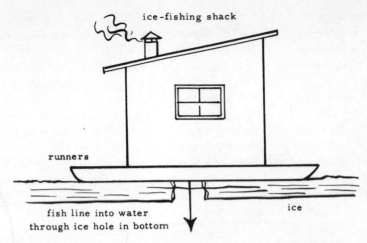

ice-fishing shack

runners

fish line into water
through ice hole in bottom

ice

around, lay the fish line over one shoulder and run madly across the ice until the Trout is pulled flopping out of the hole. As for line, the nylon bait-casting kind is best, about 15-pound-test, with a transparent leader of at least 10-pound-test. However, it doesn't work for Bluegills which are voracious feeders in summer but become strangely wary in winter. With them, use a thin 3-pound-test leader. Hooks from size No. 2 to No. 6 are generally used. Warm clothing, of course, is a necessity but some ice-anglers solve the cold problem in another way —they build a small cabin on runners, with no floor, and push it out on the ice. Then they chop their fishing hole under it and rig the tip-up. With a fire going in a small stove, they can even take their coats off and play cards while they're waiting for the fish to bite!

Bait

Artificial lures won't work for ice-fishing. A good trick, however, is to dangle a luminous lure on another line near your baited hook to bring the fish around. Live minnows or shiners (large ones for big fish and small ones for little fish) are by far the best bait. Hook the minnow under the skin near its dorsal fin so it won't be badly injured. If it dies, discard it and use another. To keep minnows alive until needed, you must have a minnow bucket with a separate ventilated inside container. When you've chopped your fishing hole and rigged your tip-up, chop another hole a short distance away. Here you can hang the inside container of the minnow bucket with its minnows. Then they won't

115

freeze because the lake water is always above freezing—if it weren't, it would be ice. Your bucket, however, standing on the open ice, can freeze solid—minnows and all!

Small dead minnows will catch some Perch and Pickerel if you keep jigging the line to give them some lifelike motion. If you run out of bait, use a fin of a Yellow Perch, or a slice of its white belly, or even one of its eyes—but you must jig continually. It's difficult to tempt winter-wary Bluegills, but there are a few baits that will do it consistently—small red manure worms, meal worms, and the grubs that you find inside goldenrod galls (bulb-like growths on the dry goldenrod stalks). Small pieces of bread strewn on the water to sink and crumbled egg-shells will act as chum and attract fish.

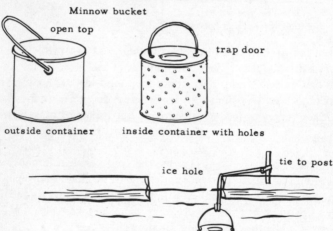

Minnow bucket

open top

trap door

outside container

inside container with holes

ice hole

tie to post

minnows under water won't freeze

How to Ice-Fish

With dead bait that you must keep jigging, your fishing is limited to a single ice hole, but live minnows permit you to fish several holes. Chop the first over shallow water near shore, the next about 100 feet out over deeper water, the third 100 feet farther, etc. Each must have a tip-up, of course. Your bait should hang about 2 feet from the bottom, so lower a sinker through each hole to determine the depth, subtract 2 feet and measure out your fish line, tying a loop in the line to mark the length. Chop a small hole for the base of your tip-up, fill this hole with

116

water so it freezes solid around the base; holding the tip-up upright, drop your line as far as the measured loop and hook it over the tip-up's trigger. You should tend your fishing holes constantly, skimming off any ice that might be forming over them, and jigging the minnows occasionally to keep them active. If you have loose line lying on the ice, be careful not to step on it and bury it in the icy surface where it might freeze and break when a fish pulls.

With tip-up fishing, a fish rarely hooks himself. His first tug on a worm or grub will release the warning flag, then the rest is up to you. If it was just a nibble, hold the line in your hand until he bites. If he doesn't after a moment, pull in because he probably took your bait. When a fish grabs a minnow, he'll first run with it, raising your flag. Let him go till he stops, then runs again. Remember, he always spits out the minnow at least once before swallowing it. Don't try to "play" a hooked ice-fish—haul him in as quickly as possible before he wakes up!

HOW TO FIGHT A FISH

An angler (he didn't deserve the title!) whom I once met on New York's famous Beaverkill River had just caught a 3-pound Rainbow Trout on tackle that would have made any fly-fisherman cry. His worm-baited hook was tied to a leader of about 15-pound-test, on a fish line too heavy to be called anything but "rope." His rod was a two-handed salt-water deal good for big Tuna; his reel could have held enough legitimate Trout line to encircle the world three times. He'd let the worm drift downstream with the current and (accidentally, of course) the Rainbow had grabbed it. Then he'd simply reeled in the fish.

"Queer kind of Trout tackle," I commented sarcastically.

"Fish don't care what tackle they're caught on," he jeered.

True! Only a "sportsman" cares about what tackle he uses. A "meat-fisherman," such as this angler, was interested just in the fish itself, not in the fun of catching it. Actually, he couldn't have known what he was missing, as anyone who has fought a similar slashing, leaping 3-pound Rainbow on a light fly rod will verify. To a sportsman, the fun begins when he's trying to fool the fish into taking his lure or bait. It ends with the fish on his dinner table. Between this beginning and end occurs that part of angling that makes it the most popular sport in the world—the contest between angler and fish. If this weren't so, all of us probably would be using hooks, worms, and hand lines, and hauling in our fish like bunches of bananas. An angler's success in this contest, of course, depends upon his skill with his tackle.

Using Fly Tackle

A fish takes a floating fly (dry fly) on the surface where you can see him, and you must strike him immediately before he realizes he's been tricked and spits it out, which he can do in a split second. Only occasionally will he hook himself. In order to strike him, there should be only a small amount of slack line between your rod and the fly, and your rod should be extended forward at about a 45-degree angle so that by lifting the tip you can instantly straighten this slack line and put pressure on the hook. If your rod is too low, a fish that takes the fly and immediately runs will snap your leader; if it is too high, you won't be able to lift it any higher to straighten the slack. The same rod position is advisable when you're using a sinking fly (wet fly) although this fishing

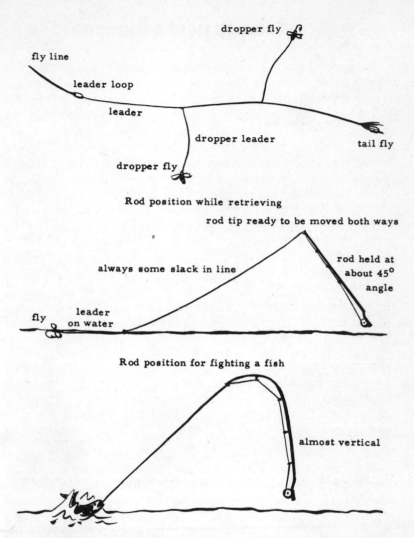

dropper fly

fly line

leader loop

leader

dropper leader

tail fly

dropper fly

Rod position while retrieving

rod tip ready to be moved both ways

always some slack in line

rod held at about 45° angle

fly

leader on water

Rod position for fighting a fish

almost vertical

is more difficult because you can't see when the fish takes it. Neither can you feel him. You must watch the loop which connects your leader to your line. Strike when this loop makes a slight movement away from you, caused by the tug of the fish. Some anglers fish a wet fly with a dry-fly "dropper" (tied to the leader by a snell several feet above the "tail" fly which is tied to the end of the leader). And they watch this dry

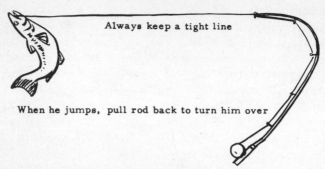

Always keep a tight line

When he jumps, pull rod back to turn him over

fly. When a fish takes the wet fly, the slight jerk will move the dry fly, too, telling the angler to strike.

The function of the rod, once the fish is hooked, is to tire him so he can be netted without danger of breaking the leader. Therefore, always hold the rod in a vertical position so that he fights its springiness. Your free hand controls the line at the reel—holding the line tight as long as the fish is making your rod bend, taking in line as the fish tires or when it runs toward you, and letting out line when the fish bends the rod so far that too much strain is being placed on the leader. When your fish tires, bring him in close, but never closer to the rod tip than the length of the rod itself. Hold the rod high over your head if necessary, transfer the line to your rod hand, hold your landing net under the water below him, lead him over it, then lower the rod so he drops into it headfirst. He may be only playing 'possum, however, so be ready to give him line if he wants to run again. The secret of fighting fish on fly tackle is: gentleness. Don't be a strongarm! That's why girls often make better anglers than boys; they're not as rough.

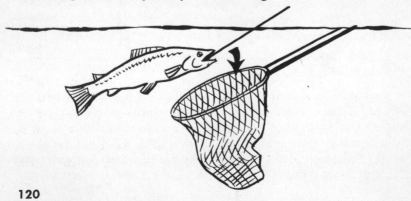

Using Bait-Casting Tackle

Gentleness pays off with a bait-casting rod, too. If you force a fish, you're apt to lose him because your line and leader may be strong enough but his mouth isn't, and the hooks will pull out. When retrieving a lure, hold your rod at a 45-degree angle as with fly tackle. And for the same reasons. As you wind in, keep your thumb on the bait-casting reel's spool, ready for action. When a fish strikes, clamp that thumb down for an instant as you lift the rod tip so that there's enough resistance to set the hook in his jaw, then release it slightly so he can run. Without your thumb pressure, his strike will make your reel backlash. Use your thumb as a brake; you might get a blister on it from a big fish, but that's a wound of honor. If you already have a blister on it, use a glove. Make the fish fight the bend in your rod, but give him line when he wants it! When he's tired, coax him in, never closer to your rod tip than the length of your rod, then lead him over your landing net, and drop him in headfirst. For fish that are too large for a hand net, anglers use a "gaff" which is a large barbless hook with a long handle. Another landing method you can use on smaller fish when you've forgotten your net is to grasp them by the lower jaw—but not if they have teeth like the Pike family. In their case you can sink the tips of your thumb and finger in their eye sockets and lift them aboard that way.

Using Spinning and Spin-Casting Tackle

The rules which pertain to bait-casting also apply to this tackle, although with these reels you don't have as much control of your line and you'll lose more fish if you're not extremely careful. With spinning reels, hooking a fish is more difficult. Be extra certain to use needle-sharp hooks so they'll be sure to sink into the fish. The problem is this: you must adjust your spinning reel's drag before you start casting—and an adjustment that's loose enough to protect the line while you're playing a fish usually isn't tight enough to hook the fish. If you don't think the hook is set, release the reel handle for an instant, grab the line near the reel and, while holding it, bear back on the rod. While you're fighting the fish, of course, the drag adjustment determines whether or not you can reel in the line (and fish). If the pull is too great, the pickup will turn but the spool will unwind to nullify it. Frequently it is necessary to tighten the drag as the fish becomes tired so you can put more pressure on him to bring him close. The change in drag adjustment is also necessary for a spin-cast reel, although with this type you won't have as great a hook-setting problem; just press down on the thumb button—this momentarily locks the line so you can exert a maximum pull on it. Netting with both spinning and spin-casting tackle is the same as with the bait-casting type.

No matter what tackle you use, there's an important rule to remember to keep a fish on your line once he's hooked—don't give him slack! Keep him fighting against the pressure of the rod. When a fish goes into his head-wagging act, either underwater or at the top of a leap, if you give him slack he'll shake loose your lure just as easily as you'd shake loose a grasshopper that's clinging to your hand. When he arcs up into the air, pull back on your rod and turn him over. Of course, no matter how careful you are, some clever fish will still throw your lure. But not as many!

And remember—be gentle! The rougher you are with a fish, the more likely you are to lose him!

Part 4—

Bait for Fresh- and Salt-Water Fishing

FRESH-WATER BAIT

Earthworms

These are the baits most popular among anglers of all ages and only a few fish species will pass them by. There are two ways of baiting an earthworm on a hook: (1) put the point into the worm near its head and thread it on, letting the tail hang loose to squirm, or (2) pass the point entirely through the worm behind its head, skip an inch of worm and pass the point through again, and continue until it hangs on the hook in loops. The advantage of the first method is that when the fish grabs the worm, he's sure to take the hook also. In the second method he can nibble off the free loops without touching the hook, but a looped worm has more action and will attract more fish. Keep worms in a well-ventilated container of earth or grass, and remove dead ones immediately. When casting a worm on a hook, use a smooth motion of your rod because a sudden snap can also snap off most of the worm. This is good advice for casting any bait.

Nightcrawlers

These are giant worms, half a foot long and as thick as a pencil, and they are also steady favorites of almost all fresh-water fish. Catching nightcrawlers can be almost as much fun as fishing. You can't dig them like earthworms because they live too deep and they crawl through their tunnels too fast, and so you must collect them at night when they come to the surface to breed. Since they like wet earth, go out in the afternoon and prepare a section of lawn, or any spot where the grass is short, by soaking it well with water. (After a rain, of course, is a perfect time to go nightcrawler gathering.) Then return to your prepared spot at about midnight, and take along a flashlight. A light will make a nightcrawler pull back into the earth with incredible speed—seldom will you find one that doesn't have his tail anchored in his burrow—but red cellophane over the flashlight's lens seems to make him less wary. When you grab for him, grab near the end that's closest to the hole and hold firmly until he squirms himself loose from the earth. For big fish, loop (don't thread) an entire nightcrawler on a hook and let him wriggle. For smaller panfish, cut the nightcrawler into inch-long pieces and thread one on a small hook. It will make excellent bait for Bass, but it's not very attractive to members of the Pike family.

Crawfish

Crawfish look like baby lobsters, 1 to 3 inches long. They are especially tempting to Bass. You can find them under the rocks in the shallow water. Hook a crawfish through the tail and always fish him with a bobber to keep him off the bottom where he'll crawl under a rock and hide. Don't be too quick to hook a Bass when he takes a crawfish. First your bobber will disappear under water as the Bass runs away with the bait. Then it will bob back to the surface as he spits out the bait to turn it around so he can swallow it headfirst. When the bobber goes under the second time, he has it and that's the time to strike.

Hellgrammites

This is a 2-inch long underwater insect that is the larva of the Dobson fly. Find him under the same rocks as the crawfish. Run the hook under the "collar" just in back of his head, but be careful of his pincers—they nip painfully. He's a special favorite of Bass and large Trout. Fish him with a bobber to keep him off the rocks, and when the bobber goes down, strike immediately—a Bass doesn't worry about which end of a hellgrammite he swallows first.

Grasshoppers and Crickets

These insects are good panfish and Trout baits, but they're fragile and won't stay on a hook very long. Keep them in a jar with a screw-cap in which you've punched a number of holes for ventilation. If you must keep them for several days, put them in the refrigerator where the cold will keep them quiet; heat will quickly revive them again. For longer periods, they'll be content to live in a loaf of bread in a large covered cardboard carton. To bait a hook with a cricket, run the point under the "collar" behind its head. For a grasshopper, run the point through the stomach so it comes out the back. With both, use very gentle casts or they'll fall off. And when a fish bites, strike immediately.

Frogs

Frogs are sure lures for the Pike family as well as Bass. The best way to catch them is with a landing net (like the one you use for fish) in which you've substituted mosquito netting for the large-holed fish netting. And carry them in a bag made of the same mosquito netting with a drawstring opening so you can insert your hand to get one without having all the others jump out. Don't use a bobber with a frog. Hook him through the upper lip only (he'll drown if you hook him through both lips), lower him into the water and let him swim off. When the fish runs off with him, give him line and wait. When the line begins to run out again, that's the time to strike because the fish has turned the frog around and has swallowed it.

Minnows

This is a name that includes all small fish, even little panfish, but more often they're called "live bait" in the angler's language. Other baits may be just as much alive, but the term is used only for minnows. They are undoubtedly the best of the natural baits for any fresh-water fish large enough to get one into his mouth. Shiners are the best-known minnows. Catch them in a minnow trap you can buy at your tackle store, or sometimes you can buy the shiners themselves from some enterprising farmer near your lake or river. If they are to remain fresh, you must keep them in cool, ventilated water. A special minnow bucket you can buy holds them in an inside compartment that you can immerse in the lake while you're fishing. But don't change them from the bucket water to the lake water too suddenly. A quick change of temperature will kill them more quickly than suffocation. Mix the waters first so the minnows can adjust slowly and without harm.

To bait a minnow, hook it lightly just under the tough skin alongside its dorsal fin, and if it's an especially lively minnow, fish it without a bobber. Let it swim away with your line until a big fish finds it. Then wait until the fish swallows it (as with crawfish and frogs) before setting the hook.

SALT-WATER BAIT

Bloodworms and Sandworms

Do you know there's a state in which raising and selling fish bait is one of the leading industries? Bloodworms and sandworms are the bait, and the state is Maine. Tons of these fish-getters are shipped annually to salt-water anglers along the Atlantic Coast. They're big worms, as thick as pencils and about 6 inches long, but they're more fragile than the nightcrawlers used in fresh-water fishing. When you put one on a hook, you must be gentle or it'll mysteriously fall apart. The sandworm is similar to the nightcrawler in appearance. The bloodworm, so called because it seems full of blood when you puncture it with a hook, has a number of legs on each side and a formidable pincer on its snout that can nip your finger if you're not careful. Buy either kind from a seaside bait dealer and keep them cool in damp seaweed in a waterproof carton. The refrigerator is a good storage place—if the "boss" of the house is willing. Use a piece of either worm on a small hook (No. 8) for Porgies, Flounder, small Sea Bass and Weakfish. Use a whole worm, or two of them, on a large hook (No. 3/0) for Striped Bass or Fluke. You can thread the worm on the hook or loop it on. Threading is best because it holds the fragile worm together. To loop one on, pass the hook through it just behind the head where it's toughest.

Squid

This little animal, from 6 to 12 inches long, resembles a miniature octopus. It is found along the North Atlantic Coast where you can buy it from almost any bait dealer. Most salt-water fish seem to be fond of it. It can be fished whole to catch Striped Bass, Sea Bass and Weakfish while still-fishing, or its tubular body can be skinned and used in strips (usually $\frac{1}{2}$ inch by 4 inches) either as a still-fishing bait or as a wriggling tail on a cast spinner or spinning lure. Since squid are cheap, large quantities can be chopped and used as chum. It must be kept cold, however, frozen if possible, because it spoils easily and then smells most unpleasant—to the fisherman if not to the fish.

Shrimp

Of all baits, this is one that no normal salt-water fish refuses. It's No. 1 on their menu. And it's even an ingredient in the prepared fish food fed in fresh-water hatcheries. In North Atlantic coastal waters the shrimp is a small creature, about $1\frac{1}{2}$ inches long, called grass shrimp or pin shrimp, but a huge Striped Bass will go for it just as eagerly as he will for a more filling 6-inch baitfish. Down South the shrimp are jumbo-sized and plumper, and are just as much in demand by the warmer-water species. The easiest way to get shrimp is to buy them from a bait dealer, but up North you can catch your own grass shrimp by working a long-handled net with a fine mesh close to the bottom along the edge of a small inlet or tidal creek. Keep the shrimp in a cool place (refrigerator, if permissible) in a flat box half full of damp seaweed or wood shavings. While fishing, keep them shielded from the sun.

Use small hooks (about No. 6) even for small fish because the shrimp themselves are so small, and hook on one shrimp for a small fish, at least three for a large species. Crush the dead shrimp and drop them overboard to make a "chum slick." For large southern fish, the jumbo shrimp can be fished whole, but bait them in small chunks for the small species.

Eels

Here are killers for Striped Bass especially, although other large fish like them also. But they're usually difficult to obtain. You can catch your own by fishing the tidal creeks at night with No. 7 hooks and earthworms or sandworms for bait, but an eel is so slippery and lively that it takes an experienced eel-angler to keep it from tying his tackle into one large knot. The more usual eel bait is just the skin, which you can buy at your tackle store preserved in jars. This skin is slipped over a two-hook arrangement called an "eel-rig" and it is cast or trolled. The water fills it, and its motion through the water gives it a realistic swimming action. If you're brave, and know how to handle eels, a small one, 6 to 10 inches long, hooked through the lip or back and allowed to swim where it wants to, is a sure thing for any Striper in sight.

Crabs

These are good baits for Striped Bass, Sea Bass, Weakfish and Porgies. All kinds of crabs are fish food, depending upon what part of the coast you're fishing. Fiddler crabs can be found in their sandy lairs between the high- and low-tide watermarks. At low tide you can gather them on the sunny mud flats if you're fast enough; they really scramble. All crab species can be caught in nets baited with dead fish. But, of course, the simplest way to get them is to buy them. Large crabs must be fished in pieces. Turn the crab on its back, break off its nipping claws so they can't hurt you, then cut it in half from head to tail. If these pieces are still too large, cut them in half also, so you have the crab in four quarters with some legs on each one. Hook the quarter between the legs, the toughest part. Small crabs (an inch in diameter) can be used whole; hook them between the legs and out the back or side.

Clams

If there's a salt-water fish that will turn up his nose at a clam, he's yet to be found. This bait rivals the shrimp as an all-fish catcher. Be careful about digging your own, however, because in many areas they're protected by shellfish laws. It's best to buy them. Keep them alive in damp seaweed and discard any with cracked shells because these will die quickly. The only part to use for bait is the neck and the tough tissue that it's connected to; the remainder is much too soft to stay on the hook. Take a hammer with you when you go fishing with clams; they're easier to open this way when they're not destined for your own dinner table.

Mullet

This is a common bait on the southern coasts of both the Atlantic and Pacific. It's a small, silver school-fish, rarely growing over a foot in length and usually taken by netting. It has almost no value as a game fish. An entire mullet hooked through the upper lip or back and still-fished from a drifting boat is a successful appetizer for big fish, but most often the mullet is fished as a "cut-bait" for smaller species. A cut-bait is simply a fillet—one side of the fish cut loose from the bones. It is wired or tied to a hook with a long shank in such a way that it wriggles through the water with a natural swimming motion and doesn't revolve. It is generally fished by trolling.

F 84